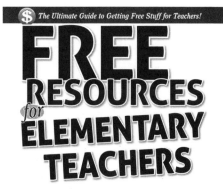

$ *The Ultimate Guide to Getting Free Stuff for Teachers!*

FREE
RESOURCES
for
ELEMENTARY
TEACHERS

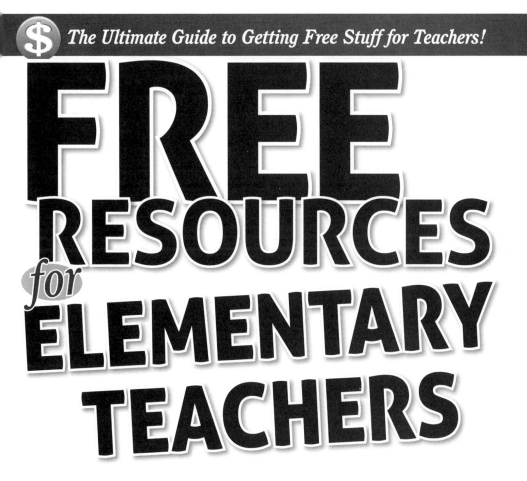

The Ultimate Guide to Getting Free Stuff for Teachers!

FREE RESOURCES for ELEMENTARY TEACHERS

COLLEEN KESSLER

PRUFROCK PRESS INC.
WACO, TEXAS

Library of Congress Cataloging-in-Publication Data

Kessler, Colleen.
 Free resources for elementary teachers / by Colleen Kessler.
   p. cm.
 ISBN 978-1-59363-863-4 (pbk.)
 1. Education, Elementary--United States--Computer network resources. 2. Internet in edu-
cation--United States. I. Title.
 LB1044.87.K48 2012
 371.33'44678--dc23
                              2011049535

Copyright © 2012 Prufrock Press Inc.

Edited by Lacy Compton

Cover and layout design by Raquel Trevino

ISBN-13: 978-1-59363-863-4

Printed in the United States of America.

At the time of this book's publication, all facts and figures cited are the most current available.
All telephone numbers, addresses, and website URLs are accurate and active. All publications,
organizations, websites, and other resources exist as described in the book, and all have been
verified. The authors and Prufrock Press Inc. make no warranty or guarantee concerning the
information and materials given out by organizations or content found at websites, and we are
not responsible for any changes that occur after this book's publication. If you find an error,
please contact Prufrock Press Inc.

Prufrock Press Inc.
P.O. Box 8813
Waco, TX 76714-8813
Phone: (800) 998-2208
Fax: (800) 240-0333
http://www.prufrock.com

Dedication

For my mom, who taught me to always
be on the lookout for a great deal.

Table of Contents

Acknowledgements

Books don't write themselves overnight, and authors cannot work on them in isolation. Thank you to all of the people who stepped up to help me make this large, and sometimes overwhelming, project happen:

★ My teacher-friends and colleagues who passed along resources they couldn't live without.

★ My friends who still loved me despite my lack of phone calls, late arrivals, bleary eyes, and confused conversations after I'd stayed up too long the night before, or tried to find "just one more resource" before rushing out the door to meet them.

★ Mom, Dad, and Aunt Judy, for countless babysitting hours and sleepovers while I worked. I'm always so thankful knowing that the kids are having fun, even when I can't make it for them.

★ Brian, for the endless breakfasts, lunches, and dinners you took over during your summer "vacation" so I could concentrate, and for all of the dishes you did solo when I went back to work after eating your offerings. (We won't dwell too long on the meatball-grease-smoke-out . . .)

★ Trevor, Molly, and little Logan Marie, who despite wanting their mommy to play with them all of the time, understood and still gave me hugs and kisses each night and lots of love.

★ My editor at Prufrock, Lacy Compton, who always has such great insight, gives creative suggestions, and makes me and my work look so much better than I could ever do alone.

★ Finally, to all of the companies, institutions, organizations, bloggers, and more who are out there trying to make learning more fun, meaningful, and engaging for kids of all ages—for free! Thank you for all that you offer and for all of the ways that you support teachers.

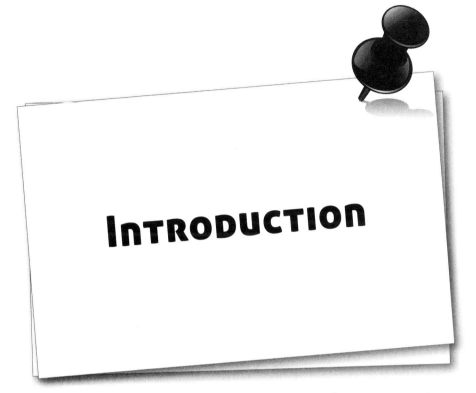

Introduction

It's summer time. Most people outside the field of teaching probably imagine educators across the country checking out of their classrooms on the last day of school and putting their feet up for the next 2 months. But the reality is different, as you know. Most teachers spend a great deal of their "off" time planning curriculum, digging up resources, writing lesson plans, and ordering materials. Many teachers spend time *in* their classrooms throughout the summer, rearranging, setting up centers, building bulletin boards, and poring through catalogs. Others spend portions of their evenings, weekends, and breaks taking additional classes, attending workshops, and working on district projects and initiatives.

In fact, most teachers spend hundreds of their own dollars and hours of their own time doing whatever they can to make their classrooms and curricula more engaging, fun, and inviting for their students. Teachers care deeply about their students and the work that they do. They want their students to succeed. Let's face it, most teachers, like you, pick up resource books like this one in an effort to make learning *better* for kids. You want them to love learning; you want to inspire them to achieve.

Over the next few years, budgets are going to need to be stretched further and further. Districts across the country are cutting positions and programs. Where there were once 20:1 student-teacher ratios, separate classes for each special area like art and music, and loads of extracurricular activities, things are changing. Class sizes are growing to all-time highs. It is no longer unusual to find public school elementary classrooms with 30 children. Classroom teachers in some districts now teach their students art, music, and physical education on top of the regular core subjects like math, reading, writing, and science.

Now you can bring creativity into your classroom, no matter where you teach—public, private, charter, parochial, or homeschool—without spending your hard-earned money. This book was written to help you provide your students with all of the materials they need to begin to love learning—without the big strain on your pocketbook.

If you look around your library and on the Internet, you'll find several different "free things for teachers" books. I know; I owned many of them when I first began teaching in the late 1990s. In fact, I still have them on my shelf and glanced back through them as I began to prepare this book. Almost all of them listed companies and other places that would provide teachers with freebies in exchange for a self-addressed stamped envelope (SASE). All you had to do to get a free poster, bookmark, lesson plan, or teacher's guide was write a quick letter on school stationary requesting the product and include an SASE or a few dollars to cover shipping, and they would send it out to you.

Things have changed a bit since those books were written. It is now easier—and more challenging—than ever to find free

things for your classroom. How can it be both easier *and* more challenging than it once was? Simple . . . the Internet. Very few companies that offer free resources to teachers work the way of the SASE and "snail mail" letter anymore. Most have an online form where you type in your information, click a button, and wait for your posters, booklets, DVDs, or CD-ROMs to show up in your mailbox 4–6 weeks later. A lot of companies have eliminated the reliance on the United States Postal Service completely. They only offer their resources on-line now. Under the "for educators" or "for teachers" tab on their website, you can download PDF files containing the resources (in some cases, the same ones that I received through the mail all those years ago). During my research for this book, I downloaded PDF files that contained amazingly high-resolution posters that I then saved on a jump drive, took to a copy center, paid a dollar or two for them to print it out for me, and left with a poster I could immediately put up on my wall (or, like the illustrated periodic table, on my son's wall). If you don't need poster-sized prints, you could quickly print letter-sized mini-posters on your home or school printer for the cost of ink and paper.

Most resources are easily a click away if you have a reasonably fast Internet connection. But the biggest obstacle and challenge to getting resources off of the Internet is keeping yourself from getting lost. It's easy to begin with a click, and find that several hours later, you are empty-handed with eye-strain and a headache. I know . . . that happened to me on several occasions as I navigated the "free resources" hits on my search engine.

I'd head to a website to check out a resource I'd found, think to myself, "This looks pretty cool; I bet teachers would love this. Oooo, but what's this?" and off I'd go, clicking on another link that would take me to another site, and then another, and another. Before long, I'd realize that an hour had gone by, and not only had I forgotten to write down the original resource, I had just spent most of my time chasing rabbit trails (or pointless resources that were more advertisements than fun and valuable learning tools for kids), and I had nothing new to include in this book. With a busy family, full-time writing career, homeschooling, and all of the other responsibilities that come with everyday living, I couldn't afford an unproductive hour. I'm sure you can't either.

With this book, I've done the work for you. I've chased down and eliminated the rabbit trails, and culled out some amazing (and FREE!) resources. Within these pages, you'll find links to complete curriculums, teaching kits, lesson plans, booklets, eBooks, webquests and virtual field trips, interactive games and online lessons, freebies, and more. Flip through the book and use little sticky notes or a pencil to mark the resources that jump out at you right away. Highlight the ones that seem like the best fit for whatever it is within your curriculum that you are most hoping to supplement or improve. Then, get a cool drink or steaming cup of coffee and settle yourself in a cushy chair with your laptop, and target those resources first. Get ready to dig in!

I do have a few suggestions to help guide you and keep you from getting lost along the way. (And, yes, I do write from experience!)

★ Get organized.

    ✓ Come up with a system for finding the resources you like when you're ready to use them.

        ☛ Before you begin searching for resources, go to the bookmarks tool in your Internet browser and set up a few folders. I like to set one up for each subject and sometimes for each topic I'm looking to supplement. For example, during the course of writing this book, I created folders entitled *general lesson plans, science, social studies, math, language arts,* and *specials.* Whenever I wanted to come back to a site or thought it was a valuable enough resource to include,

I clicked on "add to favorites" and put it into the specific folder it related to.

☞ You may be more comfortable opening different Word documents and titling them in a similar way, then copying and pasting web links that you really like to the appropriate documents.

✓ Another idea is to write the web address of a resource you like on an index card, and annotate the card with key words about how you'd use the resource in your lessons so that when you are planning that specific unit, you can pull out all of the cards that relate to the topic and gather the specific information at that time.

✓ However you organize your materials, make sure that you note whether or not you need to allow time for materials to be mailed to you.

★ Pace yourself.
    ✓ Don't try to look through every resource in this book—or even in one section—all in one sitting. You'll leave the computer tired, cranky, and with a stiff neck and a headache.
    ✓ It can be exciting to find all of the cool things that are out there, and tempting to sign up for everything all at once. But think carefully about how a resource can be used before downloading or requesting it. If you teach kindergarten, are you really going to use the booklet and poster about responsible off-shore drilling practices? If you teach fifth grade, do you truly want to waste cardstock and laminate to print and make the set of phonics Go Fish cards?

★ Have fun.
  ✓ There are some really neat websites that cater to elementary kids, teachers, parents, and homeschoolers. Explore some of them. Play the games—thinking both as a teacher and as a kid. Are they fun? Educationally sound? Would they enhance your curriculum and teach the kids something new, or are they just "fluff"?

★ Get started.
  ✓ Now you're ready to go explore. You've marked the resources you're most interested in, you know how you are going to organize your thinking, and you have some quiet time and refreshments handy. Enjoy the search. The beginning part of the navigation has been done for you, and now you get to choose from the best sites out there. I think you will be surprised at how much there is for you to use. Remember though, you need to look at resources, especially free resources, with a critical eye. Think about *how* you'll use the resource in your classroom.
  ✓ Reflect on it. Ask yourself these questions:
    ☞ How can I use this in my classroom?
    ☞ Will it enhance my lesson content (or is it just fun)?
    ☞ Will students be able to use it independently (if appropriate)?
    ☞ Is there a better way to teach this topic?
    ☞ Does the person(s) offering this resource have ulterior motives like advertising, persuasion, etc.?
    ☞ Is it an impartial view of a topic *or* can I use another resource to balance this viewpoint?
    ☞ Does it fit within my classroom climate and school/district mission?

I hope that this book helps you find lots of wonderful things to make your lessons better—both for you and for your students. You work hard. You care about your students. And you help to shape the next generation of thinkers and learners. Keep your money in your pocketbook while you build a resource-rich learning environment. And if you notice that a resource isn't available anymore, or you chase down a few rabbit trails along the way and find a new gem, drop me a line at resources@colleen-kessler.com. I'd love to know what you find.

CHAPTER 1

How This Book Is Set Up

Free Resources for Elementary Teachers is organized by subject areas. Each chapter begins with an introduction specific to that subject area. I've also included games, activities, and ideas in "Frugal Fun" sections at the end of each chapter. These quick and easy ideas can be used to start a lesson, build interest, or ease transition time. You can also use these as go-to time fillers when an assembly is delayed, a lesson is completed too soon, your kids need a diversion, there are only a couple of minutes left until lunch, or you just have some extra time.

The main subject areas are covered: language arts, mathematics, science, and social studies. I've also chosen to include the specials areas like health, P.E., music, and art because some teachers need to teach everything to their students. If you do have dedicated teachers in your building who teach specialized subjects like art, music, P.E., and health, pass along some of the resources you found or encourage them to pick up a copy of this book for their own library. Even if you don't have to teach those subjects, take a look through the chapters. Many of the resources can be used in a cross-curricular way and would add some depth to other topics that you teach.

In addition, I've chosen to include two chapters about blogs. The first contains blogs written by teachers, and the other contains blogs written by homeschoolers. The blogs contained in each of these chapters are some of my favorite resources for finding rich, child-friendly, tried-and-true ideas for teaching just about anything. Over the course of my career, I've taught second grade, third grade, and elementary gifted students, and I've also worked as an educational consultant and workshop and conference presenter. I currently write curriculum, teacher resources, and children's nonfiction full time as I homeschool our twice-exceptional son and highly gifted daughter. With a toddler hanging around too, I know the value of a great resource, and how to pick one that will enrich and help me in several areas of my life at the same time. These blogs, whether written by teachers in the trenches of a school system or homeschoolers balancing learning and living, will help you be better at what you do.

Each of the resources found within the chapters begins with the title of the web page, name of the company, or resource itself in bold print. Following that is the web address or other contact information. Finally, each resource listing is followed by a short description of what you will find or receive from the listing. I've marked some of my favorites with a smile, and all are marked according to whether the materials are printable/downloadable (computer icon) or will be mailed to you (mailbox icon). Take those symbols into account when you plan what resources you need. Obviously, you'll want to allow time for mailed materials to reach you before you plan to teach about them.

Now that you know what this book is about, have an idea of how to use it, and know its structure, it's time to explore! Have some fun, and remember—teaching *creatively* does not have to equal teaching *expensively*! You *can* develop fabulous lessons using *free* resources.

A Note About Pinterest

Are you "pinning" yet? After some kicking and screaming, along with some foot dragging, I joined up. I hesitated for so long because I really don't need another time-draining online addiction. And it *is* addictive . . .

For those of you who don't know, Pinterest is an online collection of virtual, and *visual*, bulletin boards. If you're interested in joining, there's a link to click to request an invitation on their site at http://www.pinterest.com. Once you do that, you'll receive an email with a link to click and join. Membership is free.

Once you join, you can start creating your own bulletin boards on your page. Then, while you're surfing the Internet, you can click a button to "pin" sites you want to remember to the titled bulletin boards you've created. For example, while my kids were learning about Antarctica, I looked around the web for cool sites, games, videos, lesson plans, and projects related to Antarctica, explorers, icebergs, penguins, etc. When I found something I wanted to revisit, I'd "pin" it to my Antarctica board. A photo or clipart from the site would appear on the board with a link and any comment I wrote to help me remember why I had "pinned" the site. In fact, it's so easy—and I work much better with visuals to jog my memory—that I wish I'd joined earlier in this book project. I would have used boards to keep track of my research instead of folders in my favorites menu.

There are tons of teaching ideas, free resources, links to printables, and more constantly rolling through the Pinterest homepage. If you're looking for a new take on an old topic, you can use the search feature to find fresh ideas. While you're there, consider checking out *my* boards— http://pinterest.com/colleenkessler—you can "follow" me and be notified any time I add a "pin," or just when I "pin" to a board you're interested in.

Happy pinning!

CHAPTER 2

General Resources for Elementary Teachers

From lesson plans, to bulletin board ideas, to printables, the Internet abounds with free and frugal ideas for making your classroom better. In this section, you'll find links to websites that offer lesson plans, teacher's guides, and worksheets for any and all elementary subjects. Those websites that are better suited to one or two subjects are found in the chapters specific to those topics. The resources in this chapter are, obviously, more general. For example, you'll find websites that cater to elementary teachers and offer searchable databases of lesson plans. Type in or choose a subject and grade level, and related resources pop up.

You'll also find some fun freebies that don't fit in with a subject area. I came across some great resources that offer bookmarks, pencils, stickers, or other items just for filling out a short questionnaire. I included these things here. You may want to include them in a classroom treasure chest as incentives, or offer them as prizes during review games.

As you get started planning your year, think about things you have that you can repurpose for classroom use. Or think about what you might ask friends, family, or your students' parents to donate. Things that might come in handy as general resources for your classroom are:

★ children's books that aren't used around the house anymore (for a classroom library);

★ board games (for free play, indoor recess, or repurposing playing pieces and boards into craft projects or make-your-own-board-game projects);

★ puzzle pieces from old puzzles (I used these one year for a holiday gift for parents. I spray-painted pieces green and red, and kids glued them into a wreath shape. When they were dry, we glued a photo of the child into the center like a frame, tied the wreath with a ribbon, and had an ornament to give to parents as a gift.);

★ old magazines;

★ dice;

★ paper scraps or paper discards (from copy centers or scrapbooking stores);

★ fabric scraps;

★ bottle caps;

★ metal scraps;

★ wood pieces or sawdust; and

★ other "trash" that could be made into games or art projects.

When you think about the kinds of things you do with your students, think too about what common household objects could be used. Before long, you'll start considering free projects over those that cost money! It's all in your mindset. If you always spend money on the culminating project for your pond study unit, you'll continue to do that every year. But if you find a fun activity to make with the kids, like a frog made out of the bottom of a green 2-liter bottle and foam scraps from the local craft store that eats button "flies," you'll start to look forward to this fun and free demonstration of the food chain to end your unit instead. (You just have to remember to send a note home asking parents to send in green 2-liter bottles and old buttons, and stop by the make-it-take-it section of your local craft store a few weeks earlier and ask them to save foam scraps instead of throwing them away.)

Now, while you wait for all of those recyclables you just requested to come your way, take a look through the online resources that have been gathered for you in this section.

42eXplore
http://42explore.com/index.htm

The idea behind this website is great. Its premise is based on the developers' frustration as they searched for classroom resources. Often, they'd track down a resource that sounded great, but when they typed in the link, a "File Not Found" page would pop up. This is always a possibility when dealing with the Internet. So, they've tracked down four sites for each topic, with the hope that at least two of them will always still be available. Their primary audience is students who need a safe starting point for research projects. Check it out . . . if you teach computer or research skills, this might be a good beginning point for your students.

100 Free Things to Do With Your Grandkids
http://www.grandparents.com/gp/fllpg/dnld/index.html

Although this doesn't sound like a resource you'd expect to find in a book for elementary teachers, it is definitely worth checking out. This downloadable booklet describes 100 free things to do with kids, including many that can be adapted to the elementary classroom like soda bottle bird feeders to encourage stewardship for living things or shadow puppets to teach about light.

A to Z Teacher Stuff
http://www.atozteacherstuff.com

This is a great site to explore, but make sure you have some time! There are thousands of pages to wade through—all with valuable resources like eBooks, lesson plans, unit studies, coloring sheets, worksheets, and links to outside resources.

A to Z Teacher Stuff's Free Downloads
http://www.teacherebooksnow.com/downloads/free-downloads

Here you can find dozens of free eBooks about many different topics. Classroom organization, kindergarten readers, printable file folder games, and noun dominoes are just some of the eBooks available to you. This site updates regularly so your selection may vary each time you look at it. If there's something you're interested in, download it before they change selections!

ABCya
http://www.abcya.com

All of the games on this site are free, were created by teachers, are leveled by grade, and line up to national standards. The games are fun and engaging, and the kindergarten and preschool games have a spoken component so users don't need to know how to read to play them.

Apples 4 the Teacher
http://www.apples4theteacher.com

This completely free resource site offers games, lesson plans, craft ideas, printables, worksheets, coloring pages, and more about all subject areas.

Author Jan Brett Free Coloring, Video, and Activity Pages
http://www.janbrett.com/index.html

When I first planned on including this site in the book, I thought I'd enter it in the language arts chapter . . . you know, her being an author and all. But then I took a more thorough look around. When I first discovered Jan Brett's site in 1996, I was student teaching and needed to plan and teach an author study. I chose Jan because I loved how her illustrations foreshadow or add to the text so integrally. Her site, at the time, offered some wonderful coloring pages that my second graders loved and some drawing lessons that we all benefitted from. Now, the site offers much more. There are worksheets and lesson plans for different subjects including math. There are computer games, printable games, printable math flashcards that feature her adorable animals, and so much more. This "general resource" is worth coming back to again and again.

Brain Food
http://www.rinkworks.com/brainfood

Brain Food features hundreds of games for kids to play—some can be really tricky. There are word games, logic games, and number puzzles.

The ChalkBoard
http://kidschalkboard.com

This is an award-winning site put together for preschool and kindergarten teachers. Here you'll find activities, craft recipes, resource links, rhymes, fingerplays, tips, and more.

Core Knowledge Lesson Plans
http://coreknowledge.org/lesson-plans

This is an easy-to-navigate database of lesson and unit plans from Core Knowledge and teacher volunteers. There is a disclaimer on the site that Core Knowledge has not reviewed all submitted and subsequently posted lesson plans, so read each lesson or unit plan thoroughly to determine its appropriateness for your own classroom.

Dance Mat Typing
http://www.bbc.co.uk/schools/typing/about

This is a fun and free online typing program for 7–11-year-olds. It's really easy to use, and lots of fun, too. I will admit, I've even used it myself to learn to type faster. The dancing sheep are my favorite.

Discovery Education
http://www.discoveryeducation.com/
teachers/free-k-5-teacher-resources
http://www.discoveryeducation.com/free-puzzlem
aker/?CFID=13482763&CFTOKEN=56874143

Discovery Education is a great place to find resources for all sorts of topics. The first link will take you to its general page, and you can explore from there. The second link takes you directly to Discovery Education's Puzzlemaker—one of my all-time favorite sites. Here, you can create word searches, crossword puzzles, hidden messages, math squares, and so much more! All are unique to whatever topic you are studying, because you provide the phrases and vocabulary words.

Disney Junior Full Episodes
http://disney.go.com/disneyjunior/videos-episodes/full-episodes

Disney Junior is the preschool version of the Disney Channel. Although some of the videos here might be too young for your students, some might be just what you're looking for to enrich or introduce a topic. They offer shows about folk tales, poetry, cooking, manners, art and music appreciation, and more.

GENERAL RESOURCES

Dover Publications Free Samples
http://store.doverpublications.com

When you get to the Dover Publications site, click on the "Free Samples" link in the navigation bar. Here, you'll sign up for a weekly newsletter that will include free samples from Dover's catalog.

ED Pubs: U.S. Department of Education Publications
http://www.edpubs.gov

The U.S. Department of Education offers free eBooks, posters, brochures, and other publications related to education in America. Look through the different offerings on this site and order online.

Enchanted Learning
http://www.enchantedlearning.com/Home.html

Enchanted Learning is a great resource site for teachers. It offers free worksheets, reading comprehension passages, directions for arts and crafts projects, thematic lessons, and more. Most of the materials are offered with ads, for free, but Enchanted Learning offers a subscription to individuals for $20 per year. With membership, you get all of the free printables without ads, along with access to more than 20,000 additional printables. You also get the ability to customize worksheets and quizzes. I've always found this fee to be well worth it for the amount of materials I end up using each year. Before you join, though, look through the vast menu and see if topics you regularly cover are there.

Federal Resources for Educational Excellence
http://free.ed.gov

Here you'll find resources on just about any topic you will ever need to teach—all free. There are links to videos, photos, animations, primary documents, lesson plans, and more. The materials are organized by type and subject matter. Give yourself some time to look through this site; it can be a bit overwhelming, but very rich.

Free Educational Movies
http://www.kidsknowit.com/interactive-educational-movies/index.php

Here you'll find two pages of short animations about different educational topics like lightning, adverbs, DNA, Lewis and Clark, and more. The movies are digitally created, which makes for strange-sounding voices, but the content is good.

Free Educational Posters
http://www.kidsknowit.com/free-educational-posters

Order a variety of free educational wall posters including the human body, a world map, and the solar system. All are 13" x 19" and require the educator to pay $1.85 for shipping.

Free Flashlight Carabiner From Ringtonica
http://www.ringtonica.com/aps/shop_display.php?coID=215

Ringtonica is a site that sells ringtones for cell phones. This free sample—to advertise their website and products—is fun, good for teachers who work late hours, and completely free, so I thought it worth including.

Free Online Graph Paper
http://www.incompetech.com/graphpaper

Have you ever gotten ready to teach a lesson and realized a few minutes beforehand that you'd forgotten to stock up on graph paper? That will never happen again if you bookmark this site. Here, you can make and print any type of paper imaginable.

Free Resources at Lakeshore Learning
https://www.lakeshorelearning.com/general_content/ free_resources/freeResources.jsp?f=m

Lakeshore Learning is a great store for purchasing materials for your classroom, but when you visit its website, you can find lots of freebies, too. Each month there is a different theme, and the lesson plans and activities offered all relate to that theme.

Free Scholastic Classroom Magazine Sample
http://teacher.scholastic.com/products/classmags/sample.asp

Scholastic gives classroom teachers the opportunity to try a free sample of one or more of their more than 20 classroom magazines. Fill out the online form, and choose as many different titles as you'd like to try.

Free Typing Games
http://freetypinggame.net

The folks at FreeTypingGame.net are committed to offering high-quality, free games to help kids learn how to type quickly and accurately, all while having fun.

Freeology.com Free School Stuff
http://freeology.com

Freeology offers hundreds of worksheets, graphic organizers, and resources for classroom teachers of all levels. The site is indexed by subject and resource type.

Funbrain Teachers
http://www.funbrain.com/teachers/index.html

The teacher page on Funbrain.com is a great place to start when using this exciting site. This page includes a game finder where you can search for games and activities that sound fun, a curriculum finder where you can search according to curriculum topics, and a standards finder where you can search according to national standards. There's a page that includes eBooks and comics that your students can read right online—including the web version of the first book in the *Diary of a Wimpy Kid* series! It also has a link to flashcard printables. On the bottom of the page, it further divides games according to grade level or subject level. Your students will love the cool games on this site, and you'll feel good knowing that you can make sure each game is a perfect match for your curriculum.

Funschool
http://funschool.kaboose.com

Powered by Disney Online, Funschool is exactly what it sounds like: fun and learning combined. Here you'll find craft ideas, science games, word puzzles, math quizzes, and more. And your students won't even realize that they're learning, because they'll be too busy having fun and enjoying the bright animation.

A Game a Day
http://www.agameaday.com

Once you enter this site, you'll find a current calendar with links highlighted for each day. Each link takes your students to a new game. There are two levels to choose from.

Grades K–2* Webquests
http://www.literacy.uconn.edu/k2webqu.htm

There are some great webquests on interesting topics gathered here. Webquests teach kids about research and navigating the Internet in a controlled way. A webquest usually begins with an introduction about the topic and sets a task, then gives students steps and resources for completing the task, along with a rubric for grading.

* Although the title of this page indicates that the webquests compiled are for grades K–2, I found many for grades 3–5 as well. Click around to check that the webquest you're interested in is still active and for what grade it is meant.

Great Websites for Kids
http://www.ala.org/greatsites

The American Library Association put this site together for kids and teachers. There are dozens of links to websites on various subjects like animals, math, history, science, and more.

Holiday Sampler eBook
http://www.teachervision.fen.com/botr/samplerbook.html

This holiday sampler eBook contains worksheets about Christopher Columbus, Election Day, Halloween, Thanksgiving, and more.

Kidipede
http://www.historyforkids.org

The Kidipede History for Kids website began in 1995 as a service project for sophomores at Portland State University. It was bought in 2000 and is now run by Dr. Karen Carr from the University of Michigan, Ann Arbor. She has expanded it to include topics on every subject, from history, to science and math, to yogurt making! You can find rich information on just about any topic here.

Kidport
http://www.kidport.com

Kidport is an educational software company that provides games for kids based on curriculum content. When your students go to the site, they choose their grade level. Then, they can choose a subject and start playing! The games are simple, but practice basic skills, and you're sure to find something for each area of your curriculum.

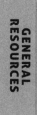

Kids' Public Radio

http://www.kidspublicradio.org

The Kids' Public Radio site offers safe streaming broadcasts for kids of all ages. Music, stories, and talk radio can all be found here.

Learning Planet

http://www.learningplanet.com/index.asp

This website is bursting with interactive games that teach just about every topic found in the elementary and middle school curriculum. Explore both the "Teachers" and "Students" tabs to find something fun for kids to do on just about any subject you have to teach.

Lesson Plans for Teachers

http://www.lessonplans.ws

This lesson plan site is home to hundreds of archived lesson plans on every subject for every grade. Choose your grade level and subject from the pull-down menu at the top, and search for suitable lesson plans.

Making Learning Fun

http://www.makinglearningfun.com

This site is best for kindergarten teachers, but other teachers may also be able to glean ideas from or adapt some of the resources on this site. There are many engaging themes, lessons, activities, and printables here.

PBS Teachers
http://www.pbs.org/teachers

PBS provides materials for use in classrooms across the country for grades PreK–12. You'll find thousands of lesson plans, on-demand video segments, interactive games, simulations, activities, and more. All of the resources included are correlated with national standards and tie to PBS programs like *NOVA, Nature, Cyberchase,* and *Between the Lions.*

Primary Resources
http://www.primaryresources.co.uk

This is a UK-based website, online since 1998, that provides resources to primary teachers. Here you'll find worksheets and lesson plans for every subject you may need to teach. Remember that some spelling and grammar may be different, as the site is based in the UK.

Puzzle Choice
http://www.puzzlechoice.com/pc/Kids_Choicex.html

This site is full of crosswords, word search puzzles, number puzzles, wordplay, logic games, brainteasers, and animal rhymes. Choose whether to access the printables or have your students play online. The online games include additions such as concentration, tic-tac-toe, jigsaw puzzles, and more.

Sandy Paper

http://sandypaper.com/memo_cube_sample.htm

Go to this link and fill out the online order form to receive a sample memo cube that can sit on your desk. Sandy Paper makes custom-designed packaging materials and provides the memo cube for free to show the quality of their products.

Scholastic Teachers

http://www2.scholastic.com/browse/learn.jsp

Although I'm sure you're familiar with Scholastic's books and class-room magazines, you may not be familiar with its website. If you haven't taken advantage of the rich treasures it offers, then you've really been missing out! Teacher resources include lesson plans, mini-books, printables, and interactive whiteboard lessons. Student activi-ties include games, interactive lessons, and writing prompts.

SchoolExpress

http://schoolexpress.com

Check out more than 1,500 free worksheets that can help you supple-ment any of your curricular areas. There are also inexpensive theme unit eBooks available for purchase.

Super Teacher Worksheets

http://www.superteacherworksheets.com

You can find hundreds of worksheets, practice drills, activities, and more for math, reading, writing, spelling, science, social studies, phonics, grammar, and just about any other subject you may have to teach here. There are also puzzles, brainteasers, craft projects, sticker charts, and teaching tips.

Teacher Created Resources
http://www.teachercreated.com/free

This site has long been recognized as a great resource for lesson supplementals and other resources to improve curriculum and motivate kids. The company's catalogs are received by teachers everywhere. But did you know that they have monthly eBooks, interactive whiteboard lessons and games, and lesson plans available for free on their site? Check it out—there's probably something great you can use!

The Teachers' Cafe
http://theteacherscafe.com

This site has it all! There are worksheets, lesson plans, and activities. You can find information on teaching holidays, reading, and math. And you'll find resources for all subjects and grades, along with chat rooms to connect with other teachers.

Teacher's Pet
http://activities.tpet.co.uk/#/Home

This UK-based teacher helper website is great! There are loads of fun and colorful games, worksheets, lessons, and other printables that will enhance any elementary classroom. You can use the activities as centers or other supplements. Remember, though, it's UK-based so money activities will be in euros and pounds and some words will be spelled in British English.

Teachers.net
http://teachers.net

Teachers.net is a community of thousands of teachers who join in chats and discussions, submit or use posted lesson plans, share projects, and list jobs. You can find "been there, done that" tips on loads of topics and scenarios you may encounter as a teacher, as well as search the lesson plan database by subject, standard, or grade. There is truly something for everyone here.

Tetra Aquademics Program
http://www.tetra-fish.com/aquademics/default.aspx

Tetra and PETCO have teamed up to offer two teachers *per store* a free 10-gallon aquarium and accessories each year. Each year they take two new teachers around the store to help them choose supplies and will even come into classrooms and do a demonstration, help your students set up their aquarium, and teach them about its care. The website offers free cross-curricular lesson planning tools including printable worksheets. This is a great offer to take advantage of if you've always wanted an aquarium in your classroom. You need to remember to call your local store near the beginning of the school year to see if they have any aquariums left for the year, or call around to several stores until you find one.

Time For Kids Magazine Teacher Resources
http://www.timeforkids.com

This site is the companion to the classroom publication *Time for Kids*. Even if you don't subscribe to the magazine, this website can be a cool resource for you and your students. There are lots of weird photos, games, lessons, and activities to choose from. Check out the "TFK Extras" tab for posters, guides, and worksheets.

TLSBooks.com
http://www.tlsbooks.com

TLSBooks.com offers free printable worksheets on subjects such as the alphabet, language arts, geography, handwriting, nursery rhymes, science, spelling, sports, and more. They also offer craft ideas, flash cards, games, and coloring pages. To narrow your search, consider clicking on the grade level you're interested in first.

Virginia Carolinas Peanuts
http://aboutpeanuts.com

Mazes, coloring pages, puzzles, riddles, comic books, and more are available at this site for you to use in your classroom to help students learn about peanuts and where they come from. There are even simple recipes, a video, and information about allergies.

Walden Media Education
http://www.walden.com/education

Are your students talking nonstop about the new movie they saw at the theater? Try to incorporate some of that excitement into your lessons. This works especially well for some of the movies that have been created from books. Walden Media has dozens of interdisciplinary units available to help you bring the messages in its movies to life for students. Each aligns with national standards and was written by a teacher.

GENERAL RESOURCES

Worksheet Library

http://www.worksheetlibrary.com

On this site, teachers can pay for a premium membership and have access to almost 20,000 worksheets. The free membership is pretty good too, though. With it, you have access to more than 950 worksheets from all subjects for grades K–8.

Frugal Fun

Activities, Tips, and Games
to Promote Engagement

10-Second Transitions

To make transitions easier and less stressful, warn students first. Tell them, "I'm going to count backward from 10. When I get to one you should have your writing journal, spelling dictionary, and a pencil on your desk." Students know what to expect ahead of time, and you don't have to get a timer, stoplight, or other classroom management tool. Besides, kids love a challenge, and 10-second transitions are like races to them.

Border and Poster Storage

I wish I had thought of this tip years ago when I taught third grade. I was fortunate enough to be in a brand-new building with *tons* of wall space and bulletin boards. I had so many posters and borders that it was tough to store them all for reuse. I bought boxes specifically designed for these items, and spent a fortune. Try this instead: Punch a small hole at one end of each border and place it over the hook of a wire coat hanger. Hang these in a closet. For your posters, clip them to plastic clothing hangers (the kind you get when you buy kids' pants) and hang them in a closet too.

Bulletin Boards That Last

Instead of covering bulletin boards with paper that tears and fades, consider asking parents and community members for fabric donations and covering your boards with brightly colored fabric instead. If you receive a large piece, you can cover the whole board. If you receive lots of little pieces, you can create a quilted look. The bonus is that the fabric can be used for several years if you take it down carefully, because it won't tear.

Comment Box

Make your students feel like they truly are part of a community and have a say in its day-to-day workings. Place an old box that has a slit cut in the top and is decorated with colored paper, contact paper, or wallpaper scraps on your desk. Then, place a stack of index cards next to it, and invite students to anonymously offer suggestions, constructive criticism, or ideas about how the class is going. Once a week, take the box home and read through the comments and suggestions. Try to make one student-suggested change or address one student-specified problem each Monday morning.

Custom Mailboxes

Classroom "mail" organizers can get expensive. This one won't cost anything but time. Collect enough same-size cereal or shipping boxes as the number of students you have, and cut the flaps off of one side. Stack them in fours, fives, or sixes with the openings facing the same way, taping them with duct tape (there is an amazing variety of colorful patterns available if you want to splurge on a couple of cute rolls instead of using the silver standby stashed in your garage) into towers. Tape the towers together to form a rectangular "box" of mailbox slots. Cover the outside with leftover wrapping or craft paper, line the edges in duct tape, and you're ready to go!

Hula Hoop Games

When your students are working in cooperative groups or playing games, and the noise and mess ramp up, try having them use hula hoops instead. Place hula hoops around your classroom. Have group members sit around the perimeter of the hoops and keep the materials for their project or games inside the circle.

Leave a Mark

I always liked to have my students leave something behind for future classes. One year, I hit upon a fun and economical idea that my students all loved. I got permission from my principal to create an ongoing mural on the ceiling. Each year, my class took a few days to work together to plan a design that was representative of our year and their unique personalities. They agreed on a direction, sketched their ideas, and voted on roles. Finally, during the last week or two of the school year, they worked together to transform one ceiling tile into a painting or mosaic that represented them. They sketched carefully on the white tile (we usually used an extra from the custodian so there wouldn't be a hole in our ceiling during the painting), and then all worked together to add the paint. Sometimes classes would then hot glue three-dimensional artifacts to the tile as well. Before the last day of school, the head custodian would stop by with his ladder and help the kids decide exactly where they wanted their tile placed. My students often came back to visit and check out the tile from their year, as well as any new additions. It didn't cost us anything—we already had the paint and brushes, and there was always a ceiling full of tiles from which to choose.

Magnetic Surfaces

Not enough magnetic board space in your classroom to accommodate your teaching, attendance, lunch count, and anything else you may need magnets for? Consider adding a few old cookie sheets to your walls. Send a note home (or talk to some friends) asking for old cookie sheets. Lightly spray paint or glue colorful fabric to them to "pretty" them up, and add a ribbon by drilling two holes at an end. Hang on a wall like a picture—then add your magnets!

Meaningful Testing

At the end of a unit, ask your students to think about the most important things they learned. Group them in twos or threes and ask them to work together to come up with 3–5 test questions related to the most important things about that unit (in their opinion). Then, create your test based on their feedback. You've now made sure they'll remember more, and made a test a meaningful way for them to show you what they know because they understand that you're including the most important information—and they created it!

Number Gems

Do you use numbers to randomly call on your students or to keep their privacy intact? I did when I taught third grade. I wrote their numbers on a variety of things—bookmarks to keep track of the books they were reading (and to return them to the correct person when a book was found in a strange location); craft sticks to pull from when I needed a reader, helper, or answer; and squares of paper for when I needed to group students. For a pretty version, try this: Pick up some inexpensive glass gems from a craft store, write numbers on craft paper, cut the numbers out so the paper fits on the underside of a gem, and use Mod Podge to adhere the number to the gem. If you want, you could also add a magnet to the back of these for lunch count and attendance use.

Picture This! Behavior Hints

Take some time during the first week of school to practice walking in a straight line, lining up for recess, cleaning/organizing student desks, writing names on papers, and all of the other expectations your elementary students have. Photograph this year's students doing these things correctly, and post those photos on a bulletin board to remind students what rules and expectations you have for them.

Portable Learning Centers

One use for the plastic cans and jars you collect is to make portable learning centers. Fill a plastic coffee can with all of the manipulatives, paperwork, directions, and supplies a student would need to independently work through a task. House these on a small bookshelf or counter, and have students take the whole center to a corner of the room or back to their desks when it is their turn to work on it.

Ready to Go Song

At the end of the day, instead of the mad rush to stuff backpacks, clean desks and floors, and straighten the classroom, play a song. The song doesn't matter—a Disney song, classical music, etc. What's important is that your students know that when the song starts, everything else stops and they get ready to go home. You won't have to remind anyone to do their jobs, and nobody will miss the bus if you train them to be accountable to begin with the music. This is a nice and calm way to end the day on a positive "note."

Storage Tips

Although this seems like a common-sense tip, I'll admit that I didn't display that sense when I taught in the classroom. Any teacher of young children, whether you teach in a public, private, parochial, or homeschool, accumulates a lot of stuff! This includes manipulatives, centers, craft supplies, crayons, and other little objects. Instead of going out and buying (like I did) plastic boxes with lids, use what you have and ask for donations. Have your students bring in clear and cleaned plastic peanut butter jars with lids, coffee cans, formula cans—really any food packaging that is plastic and has a lid can be used. If it is clear, the contents will show through. If it is opaque, like a red plastic coffee can, use colorful contact paper to cover the writing and make a label for the outside so you know what's in it.

Test the Teacher

Instead of giving a traditional quiz, ask students to read a section of their textbooks and write three stumper questions and answers. The questions must be about the content and must be able to be answered if a person read the text. Then, randomly draw names and allow that student to try to stump you. He'll read his question and you'll answer it. If you get it right, you earn a point. If you get it wrong, the class earns a point. (You could miss a few on purpose to keep the game interesting.)

CHAPTER 3

Literacy Resources

Literacy instruction represents the foundation of all teaching during the elementary years. Children need strength in this area in order to be completely successful in all other subject areas. Teaching literacy to elementary students encompasses so much more than just reading and writing, however. Strong literacy instruction needs to focus on reading, writing, listening, *and* speaking skills. In addition, kids need to work with words on a daily basis—spelling, rhyming, word families, vocabulary, games, and puzzles.

The cornerstone of this foundation should be reading. For children who are just beginning to read and experience books, actually reading is the only way to improve their skills. Because of this, elementary classrooms need to be print-resource rich. There should be a lot of books, magazines, and other printed material for kids to choose from. This doesn't need to become expensive, though.

Ask around to see if parents, friends, colleagues, or community members are getting rid of their gently used children's books and magazines. Stop by garage sales and ask if you can come by and pick up any unsold children's books after the sale to use in your classroom. Spend a little money at the used-book sales at your local public library. Often, libraries sell beautiful, but worn, picture books and early chapter books for a quarter each. This is an easy and inexpensive way to build your collection. Additionally, take advantage of book clubs. Send home the Scholastic circulars with your students. You provide parents with an easy and reasonably inexpensive way to build their own home libraries, and you earn points for any money that is spent. Just be sure that you don't spend too much of your own money on the books in the club. Put the points to work for you, and only buy when you have saved enough of them to earn free books.

Overall, writing instruction is easy to keep inexpensive. It is easily integrated into other subject areas and can be set up for independent exploration. Collect free stickers, notepads, cards, and stationary samples from carnivals and fairs, junk mail, and family and friends. Use these to set up a writing center in your classroom. Encourage kids to write notes and letters to each other, you, and their parents during free time or when they've finished other work.

Have students write about whatever topic you are currently studying in social studies or science. Make sure that the writing genre reflects your curriculum standards, and you'll be hitting two requirements at once (and making learning more meaningful for your students). For example, when I taught third grade, I needed to teach the format of a letter, the genre of persuasive writing, and about pond and vernal pool ecology in science. My students finished their studies in science by writing letters to policy-makers about why ponds and vernal pools need to be preserved and urged them to approve laws and ordinances that helped keep them safe from development.

They supported their arguments with facts about pond/ pool life and its necessity for the health of the environment, wrote in perfect letter format, and mailed their letters to real people. This real-world application allowed my students to demonstrate mastery of three separate cross-curricular topics, and showed them that they could make a difference. Most kids received replies from their recipients. This type of project doesn't cost anything (I was able to use school envelopes and the bulk mail through our board office. A project like this may require you to cover the cost of stamps and/or envelopes, depending on your situation. However, you can ask local businesses for envelope donations and request stamps from students.), and it can cover many objectives in a way that shows students the relevance of what they are learning.

Likewise, spelling, vocabulary, and other word work does not have to cost much, either. Besides the many games and activities you'll find to teach these subjects in the pages of this chapter, you can easily integrate this subject into other things you're studying as well. Have kids pick out cool, unusual, or new words in the books they read for pleasure. Using scrap paper, have them write the words, along with their meanings, and cut them into interesting shapes. Staple these to a bulletin board, and collect words throughout the year. Now you have an interesting, engaging, and year-long vocabulary study that doubles as a free classroom decoration. Who needs to spend $20 on a bulletin board set?

Finally, ask around again to see if any parents, friends, or relatives have puzzles and games that can be used in your classroom for literacy instruction. Frequent your local dollar store. At mine, I recently picked up a fun file folder game about analogies. It's bright and colorful and has really good content—and it only cost $1. At a recent garage sale, I picked up a Maya and Miguel word game for $0.50. The game is similar to Boggle, features the characters Maya and Miguel from PBS Kids, and engages kids in a spelling game that can be played in both English and Spanish. My kids are spelling words far above their grade levels and are having fun doing it.

Throughout this chapter, you'll find links to websites full of lesson plans, games, and puzzles. There are mini-books you can print to help your students build their own desktop library. You'll also find games to print and other ideas to help strengthen your literacy lessons.

AAA Spell
http://www.aaaspell.com

Type in your own spelling and vocabulary lists, and click to let students practice the words and patterns. If students need additional spelling practice, you can use the sample lists that are divided by grade level.

Aaron Shepard's Reader's Theater Page
http://www.aaronshep.com/rt

Free scripts, along with resources like tutorials, lesson plans, and research on the value of incorporating reader's theater in your class-room, are all collected on this site to make it easy to get started.

Adrian Bruce's Reading Stuff
http://www.printablereadinggames.com

If you need printable games, phonics manipulatives, or word wall resources, you've found the right site. Here you'll find flashcards, word cards, posters, games, and so much more. Consider printing some of these resources out on cardstock and laminating them, and you'll have a low-cost but pretty complete early reading program.

Aesop's Fables
http://etext.lib.virginia.edu/toc/modeng/public/AesFabl.html

Are you teaching your students about fables this year? Here you can find eText versions of all of Aesop's famous fables. This is an easy-to-use, comprehensive list.

alphaDictionary
http://www.alphadictionary.com/index.shtml

This site will engage your young wordsmiths (and you!). It is rich in puns, word origins, games, puzzles, and more. Although it is presented in a silly, tongue-in-cheek manner, there is an incredible amount of information to inspire and teach budding etymologists.

The Amazing-Incredible Handwriting Worksheet Maker
http://handwritingworksheets.com

Make your own customizable handwriting worksheets with the click of a few buttons. Choose from three different handwriting styles—basic print, D'Nealian, and cursive—type in your words, and print!

Authors & Illustrators on the Web
http://people.ucalgary.ca/~dkbrown/authors.html

The Children's Literature Web Guide provides several pages of links to authors' and illustrators' websites. Chances are, if you're beginning an author study, you'll be able to find a link to the author's website on these pages.

Barnes and Noble Summer Reading Program
http://www.barnesandnoble.com

Each summer, Barnes and Noble Booksellers offer summer reading programs for kids to participate in. Toward the end of the school year, go to the Barnes and Noble website and download and reproduce the information for your students to take home. After they read a predetermined number of books and fill out the reading record with their parents, they can go to a Barnes and Noble store to pick out a free book.

Bartleby

http://www.bartleby.com

This is a great resource for free online books. You'll find mostly classics here, but there are also materials for poetry units as well as non-fiction to help your students read for meaning.

BBC Schools

http://www.bbc.co.uk/schools/websites/4_11/site/literacy.shtml

The BBC provides a collection of lessons and games for various subjects. At this link, you'll find loads of interactive games that teach grammar, spelling, reading, and writing. Remember that this is a British website, though, and preview each game before allowing your students to play it. Some British word usages may be different than American usages.

Bilbliomania

http://www.bibliomania.com

This free site houses more than 2,000 classic works of literature, book notes, study guides, help for teachers, and summaries. This might be a good place to start if you need to teach about a particular author or text.

Bitesize Games
http://www.bbc.co.uk/schools/ks1bitesize/literacy

Short, fast-paced learning games teach grammar, phonics, and spelling at this site. The fist-pumping characters and fun sounds (and the big splash that's made when you get a wrong answer and Max falls in the water) will keep kids entertained while they forget they're learning.

Book Adventure
http://www.bookadventure.com

Book Adventure was created by the Sylvan Learning Group to help motivate children in grades K–8 to read more. The site allows teachers and parents to sign up their students to participate. Each child is given a username and password and can log in to take quizzes for books they have read. There is a reward system where kids receive points for answering quiz questions correctly and can save their points and redeem them either for prizes agreed upon and entered into the "prize library" by teachers and parents (e.g., treasure box picks, no homework passes) or for prizes supplied by Sylvan and their sponsors. There is a downloadable teacher's guide that helps you set the program up in your classroom.

Books Should Be Free
http://www.booksshouldbefree.com

Here, you can download thousands of free audio books to your computer or mp3 player.

Bookworms: Free Reading Resources for Teachers
http://www.oup-bookworms.com/teachers-only.cfm

Oxford University Press provides the resources found here. You'll find reading records, achievement awards, leveled readers, interactive tests, and audio hooks.

BrainPOP
http://www.brainpop.com/english

BrainPop was created in 1999 by an immunologist to deliver tough information to his young patients in a creative, engaging, nonthreatening way. It now contains hundreds of short, standards-based animations on a variety of curriculum topics and can be used to introduce or supplement various units. Note that it is a subscription-based site, but it offers several videos in each subject area for free. This link will take you to the English video page.

Bricks and Mortar
http://www.happychild.org.uk/home5.htm

Bricks and Mortar is an online reading curriculum that can be printed for use with struggling readers. It focuses on reinforcing the basic rules of reading and spelling. Students take a few minutes each day to look at the "disk" page while you read them the "notes" pages. This builds their interest and confidence in their reading as they then progress to easy-to-read stories. This program is based in the UK.

Carol Hurst's Children's Literature Site
http://www.carolhurst.com/index.html

Carol Hurst has won multiple awards for this site. She provides an incredibly comprehensive list of children's books, along with detailed activities and lesson plans for how you can use these books in your classroom to introduce or teach a wide array of subjects including reading, comprehension, writing, math, science, social studies, and more.

Catch the Spelling
http://www.manythings.org/cts

There are many different levels of difficulty to choose from on this site. New spellers can practice by "catching" the letters of words that are shown to them, more advanced spellers will be given a topic, and letters will be dropped that they need to unscramble to spell a word that fits within the given category.

Children's Book Awards and Literary Prizes
http://e-skolar.com/docs/media-center/
childrens-book-awards.html

This site provides links to booklists from every major award in children's literature. If you want to encourage your students to read the Newbery or Caldecott winners, or want to find out which books have won awards for their applicability to school standards, this is a site to check out thoroughly.

ChildrensPictureBooks.info

http://www.childrenspicturebooks.info/index.htm

You'll find lists and descriptions of picture books of all genres at this site. The books lists are further divided into subjects so you can find just the right picture book to introduce your next science or math topic.

Cleft the Spelling Clown

http://akidsheart.com/threer/spellclowndes.htm

Instead of Hangman, your students will pop balloons as they try to guess the letters in the spelling words you import into this interactive game. The engaging graphics were designed to attract first- and second-grade spellers.

Crazy Tales

http://www.rinkworks.com/crazytales

Remember Mad Libs, those simple, silly stories that made learning the parts of speech seem like play? Crazy Tales is based on the same concept. You can click on original stories, classic stories, or excerpts, enter in the word type specified in a list, and then click done. The story or excerpt will pop up with the silly words taking the place of the original ones.

Cursive Writing Worksheets

http://www.worksheetplace.com/index.php?function=Display
Category&showCategory=Y&links=2&id=6&link1=43&link2=6

Handwriting is still an important skill to teach, but many educators lack the time and resources to fit it in. As budgets are cut, resources that don't go along with a core subject are most often discontinued. Handwriting books are one example. Print these worksheets for your students to work on when they arrive in the morning or during transition times, and they'll have a bit of practice in making their writing legible.

D.E.A.R.: Drop Everything and Read

http://www.dropeverythingandread.com/resources.html

This site has everything you need to host your own "Drop Everything and Read" celebration in your elementary classroom. Fun and recognizable characters like Ramona adorn the materials to engage and excite young readers.

Dictionary.com

http://dictionary.reference.com

This site is more than an online dictionary. It has a word of the day, crossword of the day, word games to play, tools, and so much more. There are also links to other reference tools in this family of websites: thesaurus, flashcards, quotes, a translator, and Spanish.com.

English Grammar and Usage Worksheets
http://rhlschool.com/english.htm

You can print worksheets here to enhance your grammar curriculum.

English Vocabulary Games
http://www.vocabulary.co.il

This website is jam-packed with online word games like word searches, crossword puzzles, and hang "mouse." The great thing about the games on this site is that teachers can choose the vocabulary lists. The games also project well to use with the whole class. I played several and used a few on the SMART board in a friend's classroom. It was great fun. This site is worth returning to again and again.

Expo Writing Resource Center
http://www.scholastic.com/expo

Partnering with Scholastic, Expo brand markers has put together a great site filled with activities for parents to use at home and teachers to use in the classroom. They've also included projects, lesson plans, and ready-to-print whiteboard activities.

Folklore and Mythology Electronic Texts
http://www.pitt.edu/~dash/folktexts.html

This is a great compilation of little-known stories and texts from all over the world.

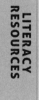

Free Language Arts Games

http://www.softschools.com/language_arts

Softschools.com provides simple games, activities, and worksheets to challenge elementary students. The language arts section can be further divided into grade levels.

Free Printables for Teachers

http://www.mes-english.com/phonics.php

The author of this site and creator of the great resources found here began this project because he was frustrated by what was available when he began looking for materials to teach English as a second language. You'll find worksheets, online games, printable games, handouts for parents, posters, and workbooks.

Free Rice

http://freerice.com

This is a fun way to test your students' vocabulary skills and do a little good in the process. For every vocabulary multiple-choice question a player gets correct, the United Nations World Food Programme donates 10 grains of rice to starving people in developing countries. You can simply play anonymously or sign up for a free account to track your progress and compete against other vocabulary lovers across the country.

Free Software for Foreign Language Learning
http://www.vistawide.com/languages/language_software.htm

This page contains a list of free (or free with a nominal shipping fee) language learning software for kids. Some, like the Jump Start Language CD, are appropriate for kids as young as PreK, while others would be better suited for upper elementary and middle school children.

Funnix
http://funnix.com

Funnix is a complete reading program available to download to your computer. It contains more than 200 lessons and corresponding activities to help you teach reading in your classroom. At the time I am writing this, the programs on the site are listed at $20.00 each. However, for the last several years, Funnix has offered their programs for free during week- or month-long promotions, usually in the beginning of each calendar year. You might, therefore, want to bookmark this site and check back once a week or so, and then take advantage of the next free download.

Giggle Poetry
http://www.gigglepoetry.com

Teaching a poetry unit, or just want to include more poems in your lesson plans to provide short writing exercises or fluency reading practice? Look no further. This site is a gem! You'll find hundreds of poems, word games, fill-in-the-blank poems to write, poetry lessons, and "Ask the Poet" questions answered. The site is created and maintained by award-winning author Bruce Lansky.

The Grammar Gorillas

http://www.funbrain.com/funbrain/grammar

The grammar gorillas need help identifying parts of speech. Turn your students loose on this game from Funbrain.com, and they'll work their way through two levels—first using just nouns and verbs, then moving on to the rest of the parts of speech.

Grammar Rock

http://schoolhouserock.tv/Grammar.html

The Schoolhouse Rock videos are collected here, along with the lyrics to each. There are clickable links to view the videos on YouTube so you can share them with your students as you introduce new parts of speech.

Graphic Organizers

http://eduplace.com/graphicorganizer

These graphic organizers, offered for free download by Houghton Mifflin Harcourt, will help your young writers organize their ideas. There are more than 30 to choose from.

Handwriting for Kids

http://handwritingforkids.com

Anything is more appealing when it is taught in an engaging and unique way. This site advocates teaching children to write not in ABC order but in order of character difficulty. It offers free lessons and animations showing how letters are formed.

Hans Christian Andersen
http://hca.gilead.org.il

This site hosts an introduction to the work of Hans Christian Andersen, a chronological list of his stories, and information about the artwork. You'll also find links to biographies, songs, and more related to his work. This is a great resource for teachers who teach a fairy tale unit.

Happy Birthday Author
http://www.happybirthdayauthor.com

Eric Van Raepenbusch, a former teacher turned stay-at-home dad, spends his days celebrating the birthdays of children's book authors and illustrators with his kids. They check out books from the library, read and enjoy the stories together, and learn a bit about the author before creating some kind of project to commemorate or act out the author's work. He shares his love of children's literature, and the fabulous activities he and his kids have done, along with lesson plans from his teaching years, on this wonderfully inspiring blog.

Harcourt Brace Spelling
http://harcourtschool.com/menus/harcourt_brace_spelling.html

Students can unscramble misspelled words in this animated game. The spelling lists are organized by grade level.

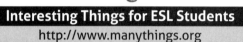

Houghton Mifflin Spelling and Vocabulary
http://eduplace.com/rdg/hmsv

Choose your grade level, and allow students to play these fun spelling and vocabulary games.

Interesting Things for ESL Students
http://www.manythings.org

This site isn't much to look at, but the more you play around with its features, the more valuable to your lessons it becomes! Although it has been put together for ESL students, the puzzles and games can benefit any elementary school student. Stick with it and suppress your first impression, then start clicking on some of the resources to see what might be a fit for your classroom.

Junie B. Jones Classroom Club
http://www.randomhouse.com/teachers/junieb

Who doesn't love Junie B.? Random House has a whole club designed around this quirky character. You can sign up for newsletters and download booklists, teacher's guides, an author bio, and an educational planner.

KidsSpell.com
http://www.kidsspell.com

With more than 6,000 words for kids to practice with, and the capability of adding your custom word lists, this might be the only spelling resource you will need to teach spelling to your students. There are spelling games of varying difficulty levels for you and your students to choose from.

Letter Sounds
http://yourchildlearns.com/dirls.htm

The software available on this site is available for free download. It is a great beginning phonics program for your kindergarteners that you can use in the classroom or computer lab. It features easy drag and drop tasks as kids match up a picture to the letter that it begins with.

LibriVox
http://librivox.org

Hundreds of classic books are available for free download into iTunes or onto your school computer from this site.

Little Bird Tales
http://littlebirdtales.com

Students can upload their drawings and narrate a story that goes along with them. Then, they can add text to their narrations. This is a very motivating way to get reluctant writers creating!

Little House Reader's Club

Harper Collins Children's Books
Media Distribution Services
307 W. 36th Street
New York, NY 10138-0285

Sign up with Harper Collins Children's Books by having your students (with their parents' permission) send their name, address, birth date, and grade to the above address, requesting membership in the Little House Reader's Club. They'll receive a kit and an official membership card.

The Magic Tree House Teachers Club

http://www.magictreehouse.com/for_teachers#for_teachers

Mary Pope Osborne's Magic Tree House books are popular with elementary readers—both as read-alouds in the early grades and as independent readers in grades 2–3. At this site, you can download activities, read articles, find teacher's guides, and share ideas with other teachers.

Magnetic Poetry

http://www.magneticpoetry.com/kids-area

At this colorful site, your students can virtually play with magnetic poetry kits and move the "magnets" around the refrigerator door. They can also check out poems other kids have already come up with for a little inspiration.

Make Beliefs Comix
http://www.makebeliefscomix.com

What a cool site! My third-grade son has been playing around here ever since I discovered it. (My third-grade, *reluctant* writer-reader son!) Kids can create and print their own comic strips using characters designed by a professional illustrator. There are even story ideas to spark their imaginations!

Mem Fox
http://www.memfox.net/welcome.html

Mem Fox is an author, speaker, and teacher. Here she provides a wealth of resources for teachers and learners of all ages. Kids can hear Mem read her books aloud, sing a book, and learn about the stories behind the stories. Teachers can read articles about her teaching philosophies and find out ways to improve their teaching skills.

Mrs. Alphabet
http://www.mrsalphabet.com

You'll find hundreds of links to reading resources for elementary students, all organized by thematic topic. Themes include Alphabet Fun, Chinese New Year, Groundhog Day, Letters and Blends, and so much more. Take a little time to explore this site. It'll be worth your while.

My StoryMaker
http://www.carnegielibrary.org/kids/storymaker

This is a fun, interactive game sponsored by the Carnegie Library of Pittsburgh that allows students to write a story with silly cartoon characters. The program helps them come up with sentences or allows them to write their own. It also lets kids animate their story. This is a great site—especially for reluctant writers!

MyVocabulary.com
http://www.myvocabulary.com

Enhance your vocabulary lessons with resources from this site. Here you'll find lesson plans for incorporating root word study in your classroom, thematic puzzles, word lists, and test prep materials.

NaNoWriMo Young Writers Program
http://ywp.nanowrimo.org

If you've never heard of NaNoWriMo, you've been missing out! Each November, writers from all genres and levels enter a writing frenzy, trying to write an entire 50,000-word novel in just one month! The folks at NaNoWriMo have developed a completely free young writer's program so that you and your students can join in the frenzy, too. The Young Writer's Program website has everything you need to take off on this one-month project including lesson plans, downloadable writer's notebooks with mini-lessons and story starters, completion certificates, and more. Several print-on-demand publishers have also partnered with NaNoWriMo to provide a free paperback copy of any book a K–5 student completes during the challenge! Can you imagine your students' sense of accomplishment as they hold *their own* book in their hands? You'll never have to listen to them complain about writing a paragraph or completing a math worksheet again—just remind them that they wrote an entire *real* book in a month, and that they can do anything!

Nate the Great Classroom Club
http://www.randomhouse.com/teachers/natethegreat

This pancake-eating detective has been a favorite of kids for decades. Here, Random House offers a printable 32-page teacher's guide to help you bring Nate and the genre of mystery alive for your students. You'll find activities for kids and resources about the author.

Native American Bedtime Stories
http://www.usa-people-search.com/content-
native-american-bedtime-stories.aspx

This is a lovely compilation of Native American stories with information and background about the tribe from which each story originated. This will be a great resource for you to use if you are trying to expose your students to stories from different cultures or if you are teaching about Native Americans in your social studies curriculum.

Nursery Rhymes
http://www-personal.umich.edu/~pfa/
dreamhouse/nursery/rhymes.html

This page includes links to nursery rhymes, along with coloring pages, tips on using nursery rhymes with children of different ages, and recommended books and additional resources. This is a great resource for PreK and kindergarten classrooms, and can likely be used in some first- and second-grade classrooms as well.

Online Word Games

http://storyit.com/wgames/wgames.htm

Need more ways to get kids excited about building a strong vocabulary? This site has loads of fun games to help you! Your students can play games and pick out words that don't belong, shoot cannons at words, and play a Scrabble-like game.

Paragraph Punch

http://www.paragraphpunch.com

This site helps users write a basic paragraph, starting with an idea and adding a topic sentence, body, and conclusion. Paragraph Punch offers a free version where students can participate in one writing activity that can be viewed on the computer but not printed or saved. They also offer a full-access version where work can be saved and printed. The free version should be sufficient to offer help to struggling writers in your class, though. You can have them copy their final paragraphs into a writing journal to practice penmanship, or you (or a parent volunteer) can type the paragraphs up after your students have finished generating them.

Pete's PowerPoint Station

http://pppst.com
http://www.pppst.com/languagearts.html
http://reading.pppst.com/sightwords.html
http://languagearts.pppst.com/grammar.html
http://languagearts.pppst.com/speaking.html
http://literature.pppst.com/authors.html

Bursting with colorful graphics and *tons* of additional links, this is a website to return to again and again. There are PowerPoint presentations on just about every subject or topic taught to elementary students on this site, along with bonus sections including free clipart and templates so you can create your own PowerPoints. I've listed links to the literacy-related ones above. If you have a projector or interactive whiteboard, this is a great site to go to when introducing a new topic of study.

Pizza Hut's Book It! Program
http://www.bookitprogram.com/default.asp

The Book It! program is an incentive-based reading motivation program that is sponsored by Pizza Hut. At the site, teachers can sign up their classrooms, grade levels, or schools. You'll receive a packet of coupons to distribute to your students each month that they participate in the program by reading a set number of books. The coupon is good for a free Pizza Hut Personal Pan Pizza at any Pizza Hut location. You'll also find lesson plans and other resources at the website. Sign-ups for the program usually occur between March and June for the upcoming school year, and spots are limited, so watch the site carefully during this time. This program is well worth the time and energy it takes to remember to keep an eye on the site during the sign-up months.

Poetry 4 Kids
http://www.poetry4kids.com

Poet Kenn Nesbitt offers funny poems, games, videos, and links for kids and teachers. You can learn more about his books and find poetry games to try out in your classroom. He's a really funny author who just might bring some spark back to your poetry lessons and help you shape a new generation of poets.

LITERACY
RESOURCES

Poets Poster
http://www.poets.org/posterRequest.php

Poets.org provides a free poster showcasing famous poets on a first-come, first-served basis. Fill out the online order form to see if any are currently available.

Printable Booklets
http://www.hubbardscupboard.org/printable_booklets.html

Print these short books for emergent readers to help them build up a small library of texts they can read successfully, or have your students read them on the computer to save paper. Each book lists the sight words that are introduced in the story. They are unleveled.

Project Gutenberg
http://www.gutenberg.org/wiki/Main_Page

This is probably more appropriate to upper elementary and middle schoolers, but it's such a great resource that I thought I'd include it. Project Gutenberg offers more than 60,000 eBooks that you can download to eReaders and computers. One way you could use this resource with upper elementary kids is to download a book from the early 1900s about a science topic you're studying and compare it to a contemporary title to show kids how literature, especially nonfiction, has changed over the years.

Purdue Online Writing Lab (OWL)
http://owl.english.purdue.edu/owl

This is a valuable website for any teacher of writing to bookmark, whether you are working with kindergarten or college students. Here you'll find thousands of free resources including articles, lesson plans, grammar tutorials, and a place to send in your writing questions.

Reader's Theatre Play Scripts
http://www.storiestogrowby.com/script.html

Featuring folk tales, fairy tales, and reader's theater scripts, this site's goal is to provide free stories for children with positive themes. The link above takes you directly to the section of the website that indexes the free reader's theater scripts.

Reading Planet
http://www.rif.org/kids/readingplanet.htm

This is an interactive site for kids between the ages of 6–12, developed by Reading Is Fundamental. Kids can play games, take quizzes, learn about featured illustrators and authors, and join the eClub. Members of the free eClub can enter contests and read books to earn prizes like T-shirts and books.

Reading Rockets
http://www.readingrockets.org/audience/teachers

Literacy resources for teachers abound at this site. Materials are available for purchase here, as it is primarily a consumer website, but if you look around, you'll find all sorts of valuable resources to help you teach your struggling readers in the classroom.

Scholastic Teachers
http://www2.scholastic.com/browse/home.jsp

This is an amazing site! Be careful, because you can get lost browsing around it for hours. There are hundreds of teaching ideas, lesson plans, author studies, student resources, games, puzzles, and much more.

SCORE CyberGuides
http://www.sdcoe.net/score/cyberguide.html

Here you'll find hundreds of free online literature guides all tied to California standards. Use these to teach units on books such as *Charlotte's Web; Sarah, Plain and Tall;* and more.

SillyBooks.net
http://www.sillybooks.net

Here you'll find fun animated books perfect for projecting on an interactive whiteboard, along with puzzles, music, and games.

Smart Tutor
http://smarttutor.com/home/reading_menu.asp

All of the activities, games, and lessons at Smart Tutor are research based and have been vetted by elementary teachers. Kids will have fun exploring the site, and you'll know that they're getting extra help in areas they need.

Spectrum

http://www.incwell.com/Spectrum.html

This is an award-winning Internet magazine that features biographies, cartoons, and activities for kids of all ages.

Spelling Bee: The Game

http://www.spellingbeethegame.com

Choose a speller, and try your hand at joining the spelling bee! This is a really fun but challenging game. It is probably best for upper elementary students or gifted kids with an interest in, and an affinity for, language arts.

Spelling City

http://www.spellingcity.com

Plug in your class spelling lists and let your students have a ball during computer time as they play age-appropriate games and puzzles, all using *their* spelling words! The majority of the site is free, but a premium edition has been added recently. In this new version, classrooms (or homeschoolers) can pay between $25 (for up to five students) and $50 (for up to 30 students) for 12 months of access. There are even site licenses available if your PTA or school district wants to subsidize one.

Spin and Spell

http://www.spinandspell.com

This is a great interactive game for kids ages 4–8. Students click on a picture, then spin the alphabet wheel to spell the word. Alternately, they can ask the computer to choose a word for them to spell. The site gives positive feedback designed to encourage kids as they learn.

Starfall

http://www.starfall.com

Starfall was founded as a complete, free online phonics curriculum in 2002. In 2009, Starfall's Kindergarten Reading and Language Arts Program debuted. This is a wonderful supplemental program for any preschool through first-grade language arts curriculum. Students are entertained and engaged while learning in a meaningful way.

Story Writing With Arthur

http://www.pbs.org/parents/arthur/lesson/storywriting

This activity guide contains many rich reading comprehension and story-writing activities for use with students in grades 1–3. There are downloadable activity sheets, lesson plans, and online games for kids to play.

Storyline Online

http://storylineonline.net

Actors and actresses read aloud well-loved picture books at this site. This would be a great site to project from your computer or put on an interactive whiteboard. Elementary students will love it.

Storynory: Free Audio Stories for Kids
http://storynory.com

Storynory has been providing free audio stories each week since November 1995! They draw on the classics and read them aloud, sometimes creating original stories or retelling fairy tales. You can download these stories to a computer or mp3 player to enhance your listening center.

StoryPlace Elementary Library
http://www.storyplace.org/eel/other.asp

This is a fun site for young readers. They can play games, print mini-books to read, and get a themed reading list to help them find books featuring topics they're interested in like dinosaurs, mammals, and riddles.

Student Interactive Story Map
http://www.readwritethink.org/classroom-resources/ student-interactives/story-30008.html

ReadWriteThink, part of the International Reading Association, provides lesson plans and interactive tools for teachers and students to use in their language arts classrooms. At this link, you'll find an interactive story map that kids can fill in online or you can print with prompts for them to answer.

Teach a Child to Read
http://succeedtoread.com/index.html

This site was developed to help parents of struggling readers, but it can help teachers pinpoint problem areas and give them tools for helping their struggling students, too.

Teachers @ Random
http://www.randomhouse.com/teachers

Random House hosts a teacher's page that includes everything you need to use their books in the classroom. There is an author spotlight each month, biographies of Random House authors, and teaching guides, along with curriculum match-ups. Resources are indexed by grade level.

Teachers and Writers Collaborative
http://www.twc.org/resources

The Teachers and Writers Collaborative is a nonprofit organization that sends writers into schools for residency programs. Their resources page contains links to many articles and ideas for teaching writing in the classroom.

Teachnet.com
http://teachnet.com/category/lessonplans/language-arts

The mission of Teachnet.com is simple: to connect teachers and give them a voice. At this link, you'll find Teachnet.com's language arts activities. These are quick lessons, games, or tasks that can jump start your lessons, beef them up, add a hands-on component to a topic you're presenting, or just give the kids a break from worksheets.

Tools for Educators: Spelling and Reading
http://www.toolsforeducators.com/spelling

At this site, you'll find fabulous worksheet generators that allow you to create and print spelling worksheets and tests and reading lesson plans and worksheets.

ToonUniversity.com
http://www.toonuniversity.com/free/
elementary-education-4th-6th_a.asp

This site has fun (and free!) reading comprehension, spelling, and grammar games.

Wacky Web Tales From Houghton Mifflin
http://www.eduplace.com/tales

Just like with Mad Libs, kids enter parts of speech in this site. When they click the button, the words they wrote are plugged into a silly story. This is great for practicing parts of speech in a fun way.

We Make Stories
http://wemakestories.com

We Make Stories is a story-creation site owned by Puffin Books. It invites kids ages 6–11 to make their own storybooks, comic books, pop-up books, or treasure maps. One of the games is free, and access to the rest of the site's content costs a one-time fee of $9.99. For this price, your students can create crazy characters and captions and add digital enhancements to their stories. It might help spark a reluctant writer to get his or her imagination down on paper.

Weekly Online Lesson
http://learnersonline.com/weekly/subject/langarts.htm

The weekly online lesson archive is just one example of Learners Online's commitment to helping teachers and families find online materials. Each week, they present language arts topics based on current events and highlight links to further resources.

WritingFix
http://www.writingfix.com

WritingFix provides hundreds of interesting and engaging writing prompts and lesson ideas for the elementary school classroom. All ideas and prompts are generated and tested by educators and students.

ZooBurst
http://zooburst.com/index.php

Allow students to create their own interactive digital pop-up books with this site, which is very intuitive and can be a lot of fun for kids from second grade through high school. Although the site does sell memberships that allow teachers to use it with up to 250 students and to create as many books as they want, there is a free version that allows 10 pop-up books per person. Students 13 and up are allowed to sign up for a free account.

FRUGAL FUN

Activities and Games to Promote Literacy Without Spending Money

Book Awards

Use ribbon or fabric scraps to make book awards like *very funny*, *best I've read*, *tough to put down*, *cool character*, *dream setting*, and more. Set up an area near your reading corner or classroom library on a table or shelf where students can prop up books that they've read and believe are award-worthy. Ask them to drape the proper ribbon on their book and do a quick book talk, explaining why they think it is a must-read.

Chalk Talk

Using sidewalk chalk, draw a telephone keypad with the letters of the alphabet (1-ABC, 2-DEF, 3-GHI, 4-JKL, 5-MNO, 6-PQR, 7-STU, 8-VWX, 9-YZ). Have your students practice spelling words by calling out the word, spelling it, and then bouncing a ball on the appropriate "key" in the correct order.

Dictation

It's intimidating for kids to get their ideas down on paper in the early years. They're imaginative and can be good storytellers, but the mechanics of writing get in their way and block their creativity. Try having them dictate a short story to you, a classroom volunteer, a tape recorder, a digital voice recorder, or voice recognition software. This keeps them seeing themselves as "writers" without having the mechanics get in the way of their characters.

Grow a Story

Have your students sit in a circle. Begin a story by saying an opening like *One Saturday night, Jenna went to her friend's house*, and then toss a soft ball to a student across the circle. Have that student add the next sentence, and then toss the ball to someone else. Set the rules: (1) You can't toss the ball to someone sitting directly next to you, (2) you can't toss the ball to the person who tossed it to you, and (3) if you notice that someone hasn't had a turn, try to include him or her the next time you have the ball to toss. Continue until the story comes to a natural close.

Guess the Adjective

Write an action sentence on the board such as *Wash your face.* Call a student to the front of the room and show her an adjective like *slowly.* (Write adjectives on index cards or scraps of paper prior to the game.) Have her act out the adjective in the context of the action sentence, and challenge the rest of the class to guess the adjective. The student who guesses first gets to try to act out the next adjective.

In the Spotlight

The next time you are having a group or classroom of students reading the same text or story with you, try this out instead of the old "round robin" reading plan. Walk around the classroom with a flashlight and shine it on the person you wish to hear read. Let the students know that when they are "in the spotlight," they need to read one (or more, depending on your preferences) paragraph, and you'll have the spotlight on the next person by the time they are finished. Have the other students follow along, because they could be in the spotlight next.

Milk Jug Lid Letters

Make letter coins with donated milk jug lids. Print several sets of letters in a fun font and an appropriate size to fit on the lid, and cut them into a circle with a large circle punch. If you don't have a circle punch, see if a colleague, friend, or parent who scrapbooks has one you could borrow, or use a coupon or teacher discount card to purchase one at a craft store. When I make letter coins with milk carton lids, I like to use fun-colored and patterned paper. Use spray adhesive or tacky glue to adhere the letters to the lids. If you want to make these more durable (so you can use them over the course of several years), you may want to use Mod Podge: Spread a thin layer on the lid, put the letters in place, then layer more Mod Podge on top. Let these dry overnight. Students can use them for:

- o making words,
- o spelling practice,
- o vowel/consonant sorting, and
- o anything else you can imagine related to spelling, reading, and vocabulary.

Popcorn Sight Words

Print or write sight words onto paper or cards with clipart of popcorn. Label a few blank cards with the word POP! in all capitals. Put them in a big bowl. (When I made mine, I tiled a Word document with clipart of a piece of popcorn, and put a square over the clipart to make a white box. I printed several copies of that, wrote sight words in the boxes, laminated the pages, cut them into cards, and tossed them into a popcorn bowl I bought at the dollar store.) Have kids take turns pulling out a card and reading it to their opponent. If they read it correctly, they can keep the card, and if not, they toss it back in. When they draw a POP! card, they lose all of their cards. The player with the most cards when time runs out for the game wins.

Roll the Words

When trying to get your students to write, try having them play this game. You need a die, some paper, and pencils. As a class, choose a title like *A Day at the Park* or *The Under-the-Bed Monster*. Have students work with a partner (or with you) and take turns writing the story together. One person rolls the die and writes the number of words she rolled. The next player rolls and writes, and play continues. When you feel time is up, warn students that they can each take two more rolls, but they need to use those to conclude the story. Give everyone a chance to share their work. Make sure nobody writes any more words than the number rolled. You are trying to get reluctant writers to write more, and by making it appealing, fun, and desirable to continue the story, you'll show them that they really do have a lot to say.

Silly-Shaped Silly Sentences

For kids like my son—a reluctant writer who *hates* handwriting practice—Silly-Shaped Silly Sentences is a fun, free game. I take a blank piece of white paper and draw wavy, curvy, jagged, or other shaped lines spread apart by a few inches. Then I dictate silly sentences like "The lizard crawled through the holes in the Swiss cheese" or "The dog meowed loudly" and have him write them in his neatest handwriting while following the path of the silly lines. He loves this activity.

Speed Words

The next time your student is complaining about memorizing a high-frequency or spelling word, challenge him to Speed Words. This simply takes a timer of some sort, paper, and something to write with. To make it even more fun, you can use a whiteboard or slate. Pick a word that is tough for your student to spell. Write the word on the paper or board that you are using and give the child a short time to study it. When he has had enough time, challenge him to write it as many times as he can in one minute. Time him and then count up the correctly spelled words. Write the "points" he earned on his paper or board. If your student thrives on competition, you take the challenge next and see if you can beat his score. To even up the odds, you should either take half the time or need to triple his score to be a winner.

Speeding Pencils

Primary students, particularly those in kindergarten and first grade, sometimes have trouble controlling their pencils to make the marks they want. Draw a wavy or jagged line on a piece of paper. Then, draw an identical line a few centimeters below that one. Have your struggling writer draw a line in between those two lines as fast as she can, without touching either one. Keep her practicing with new lines and distances between them.

Story Jars

Repurpose canning or baby food jars in your classroom writing center. Decorate four jars with ribbon and labels: Characters,

Setting, Problem, and Solution. In each jar put 15–20 cards with words that fit the categories. For example, you may have Joey, Liz, Baby Bear, a dragon, and Princess Firebaby in the Characters jar. You could include cave, home, Lollipop Lane, sunset at the beach, or a dark and scary cave in the Settings jar. Problems and solutions can vary too. When your students need writing inspiration, they can pick one or two cards from each jar and write a story based on their picks.

Tic-Tac-Word

Select vocabulary words, write their definitions on scraps of paper, and distribute paper to your students. Ask them to draw a tic-tac-toe grid on their paper. Have them write a vocabulary word in each spot. Randomly choose definitions to read. If a child has the word that matches the definition on his board, he can mark it with a button, marker cap, paper clip, or other marker. When someone gets three in a row, he wins!

CHAPTER 4

Mathematics Resources

Elementary math runs the gamut all the way from learning to count and one-to-one correspondence, to beginning algebraic thinking. Students need to understand place value and basic math facts in the early years so their upper elementary lessons aren't met with confusion. But, as anyone reading this book will likely agree, kids learn at different rates. It is not uncommon, especially in the primary grades, to have some of your students struggling with basic number sense while others are ready to apply their addition and subtraction skills to more challenging scenarios. How can teachers meet all of their students at their unique levels and continue to move them forward?

It's not practical or cost effective to buy several levels of curriculum for each classroom. Nor is it feasible to expect that you will be able to provide several separate lessons each day to accommodate the varying levels of ability in your classroom. With 25 or more students in a class, and with those numbers rising nationwide, it's getting more and more difficult to meet every student's needs.

In this section, you'll find videos that can help your advanced students move on to a new topic that is more difficult and appropriate for them than the main lesson you plan to teach. Your remedial students may be able to watch a video to see a topic presented by someone else in a new and different way. The new approach may be just what they need to help them over a stumbling block.

Additionally, you'll find lesson plans to help you shake things up or supplement your curriculum. There are lots of websites that feature great math fact games to help your students internalize basic facts in a fun way. Critical thinking and problem-solving games, puzzles, and activities abound on the web to challenge even your greatest thinkers. Many games and activities can be downloaded, printed, and then laminated so you can set up extension centers and file folder games. Or you can use these to reteach skills to struggling students. If you are in a school district that has aides or volunteers available or you have a group of parents willing to come in and help out, you can use these file folders to have ready-made activities for them to use with individuals or small groups of students.

Take some time over the summer to print the materials for 10–12 games or puzzles to use as challenge material and another 10–12 to use for remediation. Laminate and cut out all of the pieces; gather any additional materials you may need (e.g., beans for counters or game pieces, dice, playing cards); assemble everything you need into file folders, pocket folders, or manila envelopes; and write the directions in permanent marker on the outside. (You can find folders for as little as $0.10 each during August back-to-school sales and can ask local offices or copy centers to donate a few large envelopes. You could also use the free Priority Mail envelopes that are available at the post office!)

Now, when a volunteer is available to help you out during math class, you can send a group of your advanced learners into the hall with that person and a folder game. Then, after you teach your mini-lesson and get the students started on the day's assignment, you can pull together a small group of kids who need additional help and work with them.

Be creative as you stock your math supplies. Beans and pasta make great manipulatives and game pieces. Spray paint one side of flat white beans red, and you have red/white counters for probability lessons. String or yarn can help you teach kids how to measure objects that are not straight or flat. Buttons, beads, and other colorful objects are also great to use as manipulatives such as when you teach patterning to your students. In this chapter, you'll also find printable manipulatives you can assemble yourself like geometric solids and pattern blocks. Look around, though, as there are probably things all around your house that can be repurposed for your math class. Good luck!

2 + 2
http://funnymathforkids.com

You can download and install this award-winning math software for young children.

A Maths Dictionary for Kids
http://amathsdictionaryforkids.com

This is an animated dictionary for kids that explains more than 600 math terms using colorful graphics.

AAA Math
http://www.aaamath.com/index.html

This is a comprehensive set of math lessons. Every math topic for elementary learners is taught in step-by-step detail and broken down with examples. This is a great site for students who are struggling with math or who want to learn something new on their own or for teachers who are having trouble trying to break down information in a meaningful way.

Abacus
http://www.ee.ryerson.ca:8080/~elf/abacus

This interesting site has a java-enabled abacus and detailed instructions for using it for learning and teaching mathematics, along with the history of the abacus's use in education.

AIMS Puzzle Corner

http://www.aimsedu.org/puzzle/index.html

The AIMS Education Center specializes in hands-on math and science. This site offers several challenging puzzles to challenge you and your students.

AplusMath

http://www.aplusmath.com

AplusMath is a great place for students to practice their math skills in an interactive way. There is a game room, flashcards, and puzzles for them to try. You can also print your own worksheets and flashcards directly from the site.

Arcade Diner

http://www.arcadediner.com

Arcade Diner has puzzles that foster logical thinking skills like "The T Puzzle" and "Isoball 2." There are also strategy games, board games, and number games.

Arithmetic Rummy

http://www.cdm.org/kids_activities/
MathCards/MathCardsIndex.html

Here you can download and print a set of Arithmetic Rummy cards from the Children's Discovery Museum of San Jose. The site suggests that you print on cardstock, and I'd add that you may want to laminate these cards for durability. The cards themselves are engaging—each presents a number in numeric form, in English, in Spanish, and with a model. The cards can be used to play several different math games from number recognition to facts practice.

Ask Dr. Math
http://mathforum.org/dr.math

Ask Dr. Math contains an archived and searchable database of math questions and their step-by-step answers. You or your students can submit your own questions, too.

BBC Schools
http://www.bbc.co.uk/schools/
websites/4_11/site/numeracy.shtml

The BBC provides a collection of lessons and games for various sub-jects. At this link, you'll find loads of interactive games that teach mathematics. Remember that this is a British website, though, and preview each game before allowing your students to play it. Some British word usages may be different than American usages.

Bitesize Games
http://www.bbc.co.uk/schools/ks1bitesize//numeracy

This is a BBC collection of math games to teach numeracy. All are nar-rated in a thick British accent and teach addition, subtraction, multipli-cation, division, ordering of numbers, sequencing, place value, money, time, and more.

BrainPOP
http://www.brainpop.com/math

BrainPOP was created in 1999 by an immunologist to deliver tough information to his young patients in a creative, engaging, nonthreatening way. It now contains hundreds of short, standards-based animations on a variety of curriculum topics and can be used to introduce or supplement various units. Note that it is a subscription-based site, but it offers several videos in each subject area for free. This link will take you to the math video page.

Breaking Away From the Mathbook
http://sofia.nmsu.edu/~breakingaway

This is a searchable index of lessons and author's notes featuring dozens of creative projects for teaching math to students in kindergarten through eighth grade.

Click on Bricks
http://kathyschrock.net/clickonbricks

Do you have any students who struggle to learn their multiplication facts? Are any of them boys? If so, they'll *love* this site! Kathy Schrock, technology wiz, has created an interactive tutorial that teaches kids their multiplication tables using arrays made from LEGO bricks. (Girls would probably like it, too!)

MATH RESOURCES

Coolmath.com
http://www.coolmath.com

Although Coolmath.com is a site featuring math games for middle and high school students, teachers of advanced learners might find the games challenging, but doable, for their bright kids. The graphics are bright and engaging, and the games are fun. All activities are categorized by topic.

Coolmath–Games.com
http://www.coolmath-games.com

This is a brainteaser and critical thinking game site created by the Coolmath.com developers.

Coolmath4kids.com
http://www.coolmath4kids.com

Created by the same team who put together Coolmath.com, this site focuses on kids ages 3–12. Topics are categorized in the margin.

Count On
http://counton.org

This site includes a great variety of games including simple counting games for the youngest of your learners.

Count Us In

http://www.abc.net.au/countusin/default.htm

These games are designed for the littlest students in our elementary schools—those just beginning to develop number concepts. They're easy to play and make learning fun.

CTK Math Games for Kids

http://www.ctkmathgamesforkids.com

This highly acclaimed site contains a collection of math games and puzzles. The purpose of the site is to make math fun and to counter anxiety, producing pleasurable associations with math learning.

Cyberkidz

http://cyberkidzgames.com

For kids ages 4–12, this online game site allows kids to play math games aligned with curriculum standards. It boasts that when kids play these games, they'll be practicing all of their elementary math skills.

Digi-Block Sample

http://www.digi-block.com/requestSample.html

The Digi-Block program is a manipulative-based math curriculum that is geared toward K–3 students and all elementary students needing remediation. Its premise is built on fostering a connection between the ones and 10s so kids can intuit advanced problems with their increased number sense. The sample will allow you to see what their program is all about and get another manipulative into the classroom to help any of your struggling students in a new way.

Discovery Education Lesson Plans

http://www.discoveryeducation.com/search/page/-/-/
lesson-plan/mathematics/index.cfm

This site provides activities and lessons tied to curriculum and based on Discovery Education's programs, games, and vocabulary.

Dr. Mike's Math Games for Kids

http://www.dr-mikes-math-games-for-kids.com

Dr. Mike is a mathematician in Australia who has put this website together because he wants kids to think math is fun. He creates and tests the games himself, focusing on elementary-aged students, and believes that kids will learn rote skills without realizing it as they play these games.

Education 4 Kids Drill Games

http://drill.edu4kids.com

Drill practice—similar to interactive flash cards—abound on this site. Kids can test themselves with basic math facts, counting, and money.

Education Place

http://eduplace.com/kids/mw

http://eduplace.com/math/mw

The main math page from Houghton Mifflin (second link) offers basic math lessons and activities, including a math at home section to supplement your lessons. The kids section (first link) offers grade-level and standards-based games for kids to play.

Elementary Math

http://www.wyzant.com/Help/Math/Elementary_Math

This is a tutoring site that offers step-by-step, illustrated breakdowns of how to solve all different types of math problems.

Elementary Math Games

http://www.elementarymathgames.net

My daughter's favorite game on this website is "Bug, Two, Three: Math Counting Game." There truly is something for everyone on this site. Tons of games, from basic skill practice to problem solving, are available, and all are presented in a fun, colorful, animated way.

Elementary Mathematics Resources

http://www.internet4classrooms.com/math_elem.htm

On this site, you'll find a list of links to all sorts of math-related things. There are interactive whiteboard lessons, skill builders, lesson plans, resources, and more.

MATH RESOURCES

Federal Reserve Bank of New York
Elementary and Middle School
http://www.newyorkfed.org/education/elemiddleschool.html

This is a rich site with many links to PDF materials including the Econ Explorers Club, where kids learn about money and how to handle it responsibly. You can download journals, lesson plans, and booklets. This is a fun way to make learning about finance interesting to young kids.

Finance FREAK
http://www.financefreak.com

The Coolmath.com developer created this site to teach her students about money and the math associated with it.

Free Posters
http://thinkzone.wlonk.com/Posters/Posters.htm

Download free math and science posters in PDF versions at this site. The posters can print at regular letter size, or the file can be brought to a copy shop that makes poster-sized copies and you can print them there. Too much of a bother? The site does offer posters for sale, too.

Free Printable Worksheets
http://www.freeprintable.com/free-printable-worksheets

You can print a variety of math worksheets directly from this website. They have several really nice choices, and you can get some materials for other subjects as well.

Fun 4 the Brain
http://www.fun4thebrain.com

Addition, subtraction, multiplication, division, science, English, quizzes, and many more fun subjects and games can be found on this site. The designers have a way with color and are great at engaging kids of all ages.

The Game That Is Worth 1,000 Worksheets
http://letsplaymath.net/2006/12/29/the-game-that-is-worth-1000-worksheets

The Let's Play Math blog is worth checking out on its own (http://letsplaymath.net), but I wanted to highlight this page because it's a super-cheap, super-fun way to incorporate games into your math classroom. Everyone has likely played the card game War. Did you know that you can use this simple card game to teach such skills as greater than/less than, addition, subtraction, multiplication, division, fractions, negative numbers, absolute value, and multistep problem solving? This article will show you how. All you have to do is head to the dollar store to pick up a few decks of cards. Or, even more frugal, send a note home asking parents to send in a deck or two of old playing cards they have lying around. You'll soon have a deck for every student in your class! (You might even want each kid to have a deck that is permanently housed in a backpack. She can use it at school when you teach them games and then go home to "play" with her parents for homework instead of drilling flashcards each night.)

Gnarly Math
http://www.gnarlymath.com

There is a CD for sale on this site, but the free information, including archived newsletters, is substantial enough that you can use this site

MATH RESOURCES

to glean a ton of free resources. It provides great teaching information and fabulous links to other sites that help to dispel math phobia, increase math talents, and fascinate young mathematicians.

Googol Learning

http://www.googolpower.com/content

Googol Learning is a curriculum developer that has created a math program for kids designed to help them find learning fun. On this site, there are free articles, activities and games, arts and crafts, clubs, contests, lessons, math music, videos, and virtual field trips. It sells its materials and online memberships, but there is plenty to do at the site for free.

MATH RESOURCES

Great Minds Think: A Kid's Guide to Money

http://www.clevelandfed.org/Learning_Center/
Online_Activities/great_minds_think

At this page, you can order copies of a booklet entitled *Great Minds Think: A Kid's Guide to Money*. This colorful activity book teaches kids to earn, spend, budget, and save their money. If you order online, use the comments section of the order form to request a specific quantity of booklets so each of your students can have one.

Hooda Math

http://hoodamath.com

The founders of Hooda Math believe that kids learn best through games, and math lends itself well to this theory. They suggest using this site either for computer lab or center practice or using it as a class to introduce or practice certain skills via an interactive whiteboard. They also offer free worksheets to accompany your lessons.

Illuminations
http://illuminations.nctm.org

The National Council of Teachers of Mathematics presents activities, lessons, games, and links for teachers and their students.

Interactive Whiteboard Resources: Maths
http://www.topmarks.co.uk/Interactive.aspx?cat=1

Do you have an interactive whiteboard? If so, check this site out. It contains lots of lessons and games designed specifically for that incredible piece of technology.

Internet Educational Workbook
http://inew.com

This online workbook provides a large database of activities for students in grades K–6 to practice math skills. It includes answer keys and topics such as time, money, counting, calendars, and word problems.

Internet Field Trips: Math
http://teacher.scholastic.com/fieldtrp/math.htm

Scholastic provides links to more than a dozen Internet field trips you and your students can "take" to learn real-world math skills. Consider using an interactive whiteboard to conduct these trips.

MATH RESOURCES

Introduction to Fractions for Primary Students
http://mathforum.org/varnelle/knum.html

Activities and lessons in this web-based unit are aligned to NCTM standards and teach fractions in a systematic and easy-to-follow way.

Introduction to Geometry for Primary Students
http://mathforum.org/varnelle/kgeo.html

Activities and lessons in this web-based unit are aligned to NCTM standards and teach geometry in a systematic and easy-to-follow way.

Introduction to Measurement for Primary Students
http://mathforum.org/varnelle/krods.html

Activities and lessons in this web-based unit are aligned to NCTM standards and teach measurement in a systematic and easy-to-follow way.

Introduction to Symmetry for Primary Students
http://mathforum.org/varnelle/ktan.html

Activities and lessons in this web-based unit are aligned to NCTM standards and teach symmetry in a systematic and easy-to-follow way.

MATH
RESOURCES

Johnnie's Math Page
http://jmathpage.com

Johnnie's math page is a compilation of interactive games, activities, and quizzes put together by a math teacher. It would be great for individual or small-group practice, as well as for interactive whiteboard use.

Kukool Math
http://math.kukool.com/index.php?page=main&cat=tab1

Kukool is a completely free online supplemental math program. On this site, you can register, then add as many students as you'd like, assigning them each a grade level. Each time a student logs on, he is met with a set of problems appropriate to his current level. You can access progress reports for each student you have registered at any time. This is designed for grades 1–3.

The Little Animals Activity Centre
http://www.bbc.co.uk/schools/laac/numbers/chi.shtml

For your youngest students, here are some simple, animated addition and subtraction games from the talented folks at BBC.

The MacTutor History of Mathematics Archive
http://www-groups.dcs.st-and.ac.uk/~history

Here you'll find a searchable archive of thousands of biographies of famous mathematicians.

MATH RESOURCES

Martindale's Calculators On-Line Center
http://www.martindalecenter.com/Calculators.html

This is a really cool site; it's probably best for gifted elementary students, though some math-minded kids will find it intriguing. There are more than 20,000 different types of calculators to try and use from geologic time calculators to abacuses.

Math Activities
http://www.education.com/activity/math

"Math activities to show your child the fun side of learning" is the message that greets you as you enter this site. Here you'll find easy activities, games, and projects to do with your students to help them learn math in a fun and engaging way.

Math Buddy
http://www.mathbuddyonline.com/common/mbqad.html

Math Buddy's "Question of the Day" is a great way to hook kids into your math lesson. Project it on the interactive whiteboard, give the kids a few minutes at the start of the lesson to try it out, and finish the problem together to warm up before diving into your next topic. On this site, you'll also find interactive online worksheets and activities.

Math Cats
http://www.mathcats.com

This is the entry portal to a "land of creative, open-ended math exploration." Here, your students can explore, learn math crafts, and visit the art gallery, and you can check out the "4 Older Cats" section. There you'll find information about the site and have an opportunity to sign up for a free newsletter.

Math Central
http://mathcentral.uregina.ca/index.php

Math Central is run by teachers and students at the University of Regina in Regina, Saskatchewan, Canada. It has won numerous awards since its launch in 1995. You'll find teaching ideas and a glossary of mathematical terms in the "Resource Room," mathematical questions answered by real-life mathematicians in "Quandaries and Queries," math careers in "Mathematics With a Human Face," and a problem of the month in "Math Beyond School."

Math Concepts, Tips, Games, and Worksheets
http://www.softschools.com/math

Softschools.com provides simple games, activities, and worksheets to challenge elementary students. The math section can be further divided into grade levels.

Math Doodles
http://www.carstensstudios.com/mathdoodles/
mathdoodlesDemos.htm

The author proclaims that it wasn't until after he left school that he made the realization that math was fun. This site features some demos of games he's created as apps for the iPod or iPad. I like the Hydro Maze, though it took a little time before I got the hang of it.

MATH RESOURCES

The Math Explorer

http://www.exploratorium.edu/publications/math_explorer

This site, powered by the Museum of Science, Art, and Human Perception, has games, crafts, experiments, and more for kids of all ages. There is a searchable database that can help you find information on whatever you're looking to teach.

Math Fun

http://www.educationworld.com/a_lesson/
lesson/lesson265.shtml

This Education World page hosts an article describing "invisible math," so named because kids won't know they're learning math—they'll think they're just playing games. There are five lessons, each with additional web links to enhance the content. Several games are for learners third grade and above, and two can be used with kids as young as PreK.

Math Games for Elementary and Middle School

http://www.free-training-tutorial.com/math-games.html

This is an online compilation of math games for kids in grades 2–4. Here, your students can click on a topic, and they'll be able to play several different games that practice or test that skill. All games have been vetted by math teachers.

MATH RESOURCES

Math Is Fun
http://www.mathsisfun.com

This is a collection of games, resources, worksheets, and lessons covering topics such as data, geometry, numbers, and math vocabulary.

Maths Is Good For You
http://mathisgoodforyou.com

This website is updated regularly and features materials related to the history of mathematics. Lessons are available to accompany each topic, along with worksheets, timelines, and presentations.

Math Lessons Today!
http://www.math-lessons.ca/index.html

Students can explore times tables, fractions, and decimals through a variety of worksheets, tutorials, and games on this site.

Math Nook
http://www.mathnook.com

The math games on this site are fabulous! You can find games that reinforce rounding, money, geometry, math vocabulary, bus driver math, and more. It's easy to lose track of time here!

Math Playground
http://www.mathplayground.com

I love the tagline on this website: Online Math Games That Give Your Brain a Workout! Isn't that what we all hope for our students? Brain workouts (learning) while having fun playing games! Here your students can play in the "Stay Sharp Arcade," try flashcards to sharpen their skills, print worksheets, and play with online manipulatives.

MathEbook.net
http://www.mathebook.net/elementary.htm

If your budget is tight, this site may really help you out. Instead of buying consumable workbooks or printing worksheets, consider trying out interactive eWorkbooks. You can choose from any elementary math topic, and then click on the virtual or eWorkbook options. The virtual option will allow your students to solve their problems in a game-like way, checking their own work. The eWorkbook option will bring up a writeable PDF that your students can file on the computer for you to grade later or print a copy if you still need the paper accountability.

Mathematical Experiments
http://www.hunkinsexperiments.com/themes/themes_maths.htm

Part of Hunkin's Experiments, this site contains activities and experiments for students to use to play around with math. Kids will have fun proving that 1 = 2 and 2 = 3!

Mathematical Matching Puzzles
http://www.interactivestuff.org/match/math.phtml

These matching puzzles can be used for fun or as online, interactive flashcards to help reinforce math facts with your students.

Mathematics
http://learner.org/resources/browse.html?discipline=5

From the Annenberg Foundation, this site provides an index of videos about how to teach just about any math subject from simple measurement to advanced calculus. There are online video workshops for teachers, as well as videos that students would benefit from. It may take you a while to navigate the site at first, but you'll find some gems here.

Mathematics Lessons That Are Fun! Fun! Fun!
http://math.rice.edu/~lanius/Lessons

Cynthia Lanius, a former math professor at Rice University who is now doing international consulting work in the field of mathematics, created this award-winning site. There are tons of interactive math lessons for kids like "Who Wants Pizza?," Let's Graph!," and "Calendar Fun: It's Algebra."

Mathematics Worksheets

http://www.worksheetgenius.com/html/
mathematics_worksheets.php

This site features different types of math worksheets to choose from. With the click of a few buttons, you'll have a worksheet tailored to whatever it is you are currently teaching.

MathFLIX

http://mathflix.luc.edu

MathFLIX is a site maintained by Loyola University in Chicago. It contains more than 1,000 short Quicktime video segments that teach math skills aligned with NCTM standards. Most of these segments come from a television program called "Countdown" that was once broadcast weekly to Chicago-area schools.

Mathmaster

http://mathmaster.org

Mathmaster is a free resource for teachers and students. The site offers a comprehensive video library and hundreds of printable worksheets. The math videos are short and easy to comprehend, and the worksheets are customizable.

Maths for Kids

http://www.math-exercises-for-kids.com

Maths for Kids is designed for kids ages 6–11. Your students can access math exercises by choosing from 10 different levels.

Mathwire
http://mathwire.com

This is a blog written by a teacher. She shares standards-based activities, games, and worksheets. You can follow by the date of the blog post, or go to the index to find subjects and topics that you are looking for.

Multiplication Rock and Money Rock
http://schoolhouserock.tv/Multiplication.html
http://schoolhouserock.tv/Money.html

The Schoolhouse Rock videos are collected here, along with the lyrics to each. There are clickable links to view the videos on YouTube so you can share them with your students as you introduce new topics about math.

MATH RESOURCES

Mr. Nussbaum's Math Lab
http://www.mrnussbaum.com/mathcode.htm

Originally started as a class website, Mr. Nussbaum's site has grown to thousands of pages. He creates crazy, unique, and fun games for kids and is passionate about making learning fun. All of the games on the website are free, but he does sell his games as apps through iTunes as well.

Nick's Mathematical Miscellany
http://www.qbyte.org

Resources, links, and puzzles fill this page. You can find something about most math topics by checking out this page first.

NumberNut
http://numbernut.com

You'll find everything you could ever need for math here—activities, lessons, quizzes, and games that cover all areas: shapes, colors, counting, numbers, addition, subtraction, multiplication, division, order of operations, dates, time, fractions, decimals, percentages, estimation, rounding, ratios, money, and much more!

Numbers: Facts, Figures, and Fiction
http://www.richardphillips.org.uk/number

Richard Phillips, author of *Numbers: Facts, Figures, and Fiction*, has put together this website to promote his book. There is a cool (and free) application on the site, however, that is great for calendar time in an elementary classroom. If you click on a date on the 31-day calendar, you'll find a set of facts about that number. Some numbers have more information than others, and some of the facts may not make sense to very young children, but there is a lot that can be mined from this site.

On-Line Math Worksheet Generator
http://themathworksheetsite.com

This worksheet generator can create printables with all basic operations, fractions, decimals, and more.

Pattern Blocks

http://ejad.best.vwh.net/java/patterns/patterns_j.shtml

This cool site would be great for use with an interactive whiteboard. You are given a blank panel and can drag pattern blocks to form shapes and represent different types of fractions. If you can't figure out how to work it or want some suggestions for its use, click on either the instructions or descriptions link on the bottom of the page.

Pete's PowerPoint Station

http://math.pppst.com/index.html

Bursting with colorful graphics and *tons* of additional links, this is a website to return to again and again. PowerPoint presentations on just about every subject or topic taught to elementary students can be found at this site, along with bonus sections including free clipart and templates so you can create your own PowerPoints. If you have a projector or interactive whiteboard, this is a great site to go to when introducing a new topic of study.

MATH RESOURCES

Pi Poster

http://unihedron.com/projects/pi

How many digits of pi can you recite? This is the question that the folks at Unihedron ask. They offer a free 8 1/2" x 11" download of the pi poster, and offer a full-size poster for purchase at their site.

PrimaryGames Curriculum Guide: Math
http://www.primarygames.com/curriculum/math.htm

Starting off with a chart showing which games cover each math skill, this is an easy site to use and navigate. The games and activities are fun and engaging for kids, too.

PuzzlePicnic
http://www.puzzlepicnic.com

Critical and logical thinking are an important component, not only in math learning, but in learning in general. Kids need to be taught thinking skills, but your days as a teacher are already jammed with other things. This site is a good way to quickly expose your kids to logic.

Reproducible Materials
http://www.decimalsquares.com/repromaterials.html

If you ever run out of graph paper and need some quickly, this is the page to know about. Here you can click on several links and bring up different styles of graph and decimal paper.

Rick's Math Web
http://www.ricksmath.com

Originally started to help out some of the creator's students, this site has continued to grow. Here you'll find tutorials about every subject in math, along with free printable worksheets to reinforce what students learn on the site. This website is constantly being updated.

Sheppard Software Math

http://www.sheppardsoftware.com/math.htm

Powered by Sheppard Software, this page is full of links to games that help teach all levels of elementary math. It even boasts some online strategy and thinking games like Mahjong.

Skillswise + Maths

http://www.bbc.co.uk/skillswise/numbers/wholenumbers

Click on any of the tabs at this resource from the BBC for quick courses in whole numbers, measuring, fractions, and other math topics. This is a great site for remediating and teaching math literacy to older learners. Some of the additional links go to games and quizzes.

Solve My Math

http://www.solvemymath.com/math_games

This page is filled with fun, interesting, and educational games to teach most math subjects. I love that they include many logic and critical-thinking skills games.

Symbols on American Money

http://www.philadelphiafed.org/education/teachers/
publications/symbols-on-american-money

This is a great web page! It's long and includes a lot of text, so you may want to print it out and break it down for younger kids, maybe making transparencies of some of the images or information. But it's well worth the time you take to do that. The Federal Reserve Bank of Philadelphia put a lot of time into describing the symbolism on American paper money throughout time.

Teachnet.com
http://teachnet.com/category/lessonplans/math

The mission of Teachnet.com is simple: to connect teachers and give them a voice. At this link, you'll find Teachnet.com's math activities. These are quick lessons, games, or tasks that can jump start your lessons, beef them up, add a hands-on component to a topic you're presenting, or just give the kids a break from worksheets.

Terry's Puzzles
http://www.terrystickels.com/puzzles.html

Author Terry Stickels is a speaker and creative problem solver. He dedicates his life to fostering these skills in kids and making it fun. On his site, you'll find downloadable PDFs that feature several fun and challenging puzzles to test your sharpest math minds.

WebMath
http://www.webmath.com

You need to send this link home to every parent of every student in your school! WebMath is an online math help site that works with your students to help them understand virtually any math concept they're stuck on. They just type a problem into the help box, and a mini-lesson pops up in real time, teaching them the steps that need to be taken to arrive at the correct answer.

Weekly Online Lessons

http://www.learnersonline.com/weekly/subject/math.htm

The weekly online lesson archive is just one example of Learners Online's commitment to helping teachers and families find online materials. Each week, it presents math topics based on current events and highlights links to further resources.

XP Math

http://www.xpmath.com

This comprehensive site has math games to encourage, challenge, and teach kids from elementary school math to advanced high school math. At this site, you'll also find downloadable eBooks and videos.

MATH RESOURCES

FRUGAL FUN

Activities and Games to Promote Math Without Spending Money

Calculator Hop

Draw a calculator outside with sidewalk chalk. On her turn, a player tosses her marker on 1, then completes a math equation to equal it. For example, she might toss a beanbag on 1 and say (while hopping), "1 = 5 − 4." If the equation is correct, the player advances to the next number on her next turn. If it is incorrect, or she steps on the wrong "button" or on a line, her turn is over and she must start at 1 on the next turn. The first one to complete equations for 1–9 wins.

Checkers . . . With a Twist!

Apply numbered dot stickers to the pieces in a checkers set. Play the game as you normally would, but when a player jumps another player, he must multiply the two numbers. If the product is correct he earns that number in points. If not, he loses his turn. Play continues until it would normally end, but the winner is the person with the highest number of points.

Class Store

Stick some price tags on donated toys and play food, gather some donated play money (potentially from old games), and have your students "buy and sell" with each other during play or free time. This game is not only for the very young. Oftentimes we relegate role-playing games to kindergarten classrooms and forget that third and fourth graders like to be silly too. If any older students seem reserved about playing, jump in yourself and play it up. They'll shake loose, have fun, and learn about adding and subtracting money, sticking to a budget, sales tax, and percent-off sales.

Estimation Jar

This is one of the simplest and most effective activities I ever used in my classroom. On the first full week of school I would place a clear (clean) peanut butter jar filled with bouncy balls on my desk. Then, I'd walk around the room and place a sticky note on each desk and tell students that they had until Wednesday to check out the jar and make an estimate about how many balls were in it and write their guess and name on the note. I'd pass the jar around, and then place it on my desk where anyone could walk up and look at it throughout the week. On Wednesday afternoon, we'd take 10 minutes and arrange the sticky note estimates on the board in a number line. We'd talk about the *range* of guesses, the *highest* and *lowest* guesses, and any *outliers*. Then, I'd randomly choose two students to count the contents in the front of the room while we sat on the floor around them. The student with the closest estimate to the actual number took the empty jar home and filled it with items for the next week. If that student had already taken the jar, he or she would choose someone else. The kids all loved it, and it didn't cost me anything but a few pads of sticky notes and 15–20 minutes a week. In the interest of time (and sanity!) you may want to employ the caveat that items must be of a certain size or larger. You don't want to spend the afternoon counting the grains of rice that one of your more creative thinkers brought in!

How Much Is Your Pasta Worth?

Fill a big bowl with several different shapes of pasta. Tape one of each shape to the board and put an equal sign and a value next to it. For example, bowtie pasta might be worth 12, ziti might be worth 17, and wagon wheels might be worth 25. Or, if you're working with primary kids, your values might be single digits. Have students scoop 1/2 cup of pasta onto a paper plate and add up the value of their "plate of pasta." This game can be played over and over again with the same plates and pasta; you can even set it up as an independent center. Pasta regularly goes on sale for as little as $0.50 a box, paper plates are inexpensive, and measuring cups are often found in the dollar store or dollar section at Target. (Or you could ask parents to send in pasta, plates, and old measuring cups!) The materials are likely to cost only a few dollars, and the game can be used for years.

The Lot Is Full

On a piece of cardboard, draw a parking lot filled with enough spaces to accommodate play cars. Label the cars with either a colored dot or a shape sticker. Each player chooses a color or shape to represent him or her. Number each space to correspond to answers to math problems you want your students to remember. Create two sets of craft sticks with the numbers 0–12 (or whatever range your students are working on in math). Have students choose two sticks and add (or multiply) to find out where to park the first car. Continue play, alternating until all of the spaces are filled. If a student finds an answer and the space is already filled, she cannot place a car on that turn. The player with the most parked cars wins.

Math Lids

Using a rectangular shoebox (or similar) lid, write numbers along the perimeter with a permanent black marker. Write the same numbers on slips of paper and place them facedown on a table or in a bowl. Write operation symbols on dot stickers and cover the spots on a die with them. Have students choose two number slips, and mark them with a paperclip or bingo marker on the lid. Then, have them roll the die to see what operation they need to use on the two numbers. If they get the correct answer, they earn a point and go again, and if not, their turn is over. This can be used simply as a review tool if you'd rather not use it competitively.

Play Games

Math skills are taught often in games kids already love. Send a list home at the beginning of the year asking parents if they, or their extended families, have any of the following games (or any others you can think of) that they'd be willing to donate to the classroom for a weekly or monthly "Game Day":

- Uno
- Yahtzee
- Rummikub
- Dominoes
- 24
- Sequence
- Muggins
- Mancala
- Blokus
- Monopoly

Race to 500

Have your students roll two dice and add the numbers. Then, have them roll again, adding the new sum to the previous one. Continue until they reach 500. How many rolls did it take?

Simple Balance Scales

If you don't have a set of balance scales and need one for your upcoming measurement unit, try this: Suspend a wire coat hanger from the ceiling or a cabinet and hook two paper cups, one to each side, with paper clips.

Swatter Math

Pick up a couple of fly swatters (I found two for $1 at the dollar store). Draw a grid on the board and write in answers to addition, subtraction, multiplication, and division problems. Group the class into two teams. Call one player up from each team, have him or her face the board with a flyswatter, and call out a math problem. The first player to swat the correct answer wins a point for his or her team.

Yummy Manipulatives

Kids love novel ideas, and while using candy and cereal pieces to do math isn't a new idea, it will seem so to them. Use different colored cereal or candy pieces to teach students how to classify (sort), graph, compare greater than and less than, add, subtract, multiply, and divide. Different states and different schools have different policies about this, so check with your administrator before you use food in the classroom.

CHAPTER 5

Science Resources

Science helps kids learn to think critically and creatively. It helps them understand their world and gives them permission to ask questions when something doesn't make sense. Science also helps kids get comfortable with the possibility that all of the answers might not be known, but that there is always something new to discover. When children learn to question, and then find out the answers on their own, they internalize and appreciate learning more.

However, it is getting more and more difficult to teach science on a regular basis in the elementary classroom. Testing focuses primarily on reading and math instruction, and after preparing students for high-stakes testing, teachers have very little time left over to sneak in "fun stuff" like science experiments. Science education is sometimes intimidating to teachers, too. Often, teachers (really, anyone) can be nervous about presenting a demonstration that may not turn out the way it's supposed to. Unexpected results happen all of the time in the sciences and lead to new and more exciting questions. But in an elementary lesson, we often want everything to turn out perfectly. Be daring—and be willing to fail! You'll teach your students incredible lessons this way.

The trick, too, is to integrate content areas like science, social studies, and health into reading and math whenever possible. Do a teacher demonstration of a simple science experiment, and then set up centers around the room for students to explore when they have free time. Have a class "museum" area that is set up with magnifying glasses, microscopes, and specimens like seed pods, leaves, bark, cocoons, and insect egg casings. Encourage students to read about these specimens by leaving out books and field guides on those subjects. Put a pair of children's binoculars by a window and some birdfeeders in the yard for kids to observe.

Depending on your school policy, consider having a classroom pet, aquarium, or collection of plants. Not only do these give the room a more inviting feel, they help teach students to appreciate living things and care for others. Plants and pets require care and special handling, so make sure you know what is required and be prepared to take over if your students aren't ready to take care of them on their own. Teach them how to respect the animals and their needs, and find safe homes for your living additions during school vacations and weekends. Never leave pets unattended for long periods of time.

Pets and plants can be found for free or inexpensive when you start asking around, too. I taught in a classroom setting or in a gifted resource room for more than 10 years. Every year I had pets. Rarely did they cost me anything to maintain or acquire, and they were always happy, healthy, and well cared for. Over the years, I had hamsters, mice, guinea pigs, fish, hermit crabs, a turtle, and a tarantula, and every year I hosted a slew of tadpoles that happily turned into frogs before hopping back into the pond they were scooped from.

Once other teachers and parents knew that my students and I would care for all manner of pets, we would regularly receive e-mails asking if we wanted to take an animal or insect that was found or couldn't be cared for any longer. We always said yes and cared for them until they found new homes or became a permanent part of the classroom. The local pet store gladly gave us lessons on how to care for our various friends, and a veterinarian-parent of a student cared (for free) for a pregnant guinea pig someone had dropped off in my room unexpectedly one day (and he cared for every other animal I had long after his son left my room). Lily was a favorite of my students, well taken care of, and had five beautiful babies that were all happily adopted out. The kids learned life science, responsibility, and compassion from those animals, and eagerly read to them, watched them to calm their fears and stress, and wrote some really funny stories about them. They also learned to keep a nature journal and honed their observation skills.

Science doesn't have to be expensive; it has to be accessible and engaging. This chapter is loaded with freebies. There are posters to order or print that may inspire a future Einstein. You can project some of the free videos or games on an interactive whiteboard or a projector to get all of the kids involved in the topic. Or try setting up a classroom "science computer." Each week, bookmark one of the games in this chapter that relates to whatever topic you're studying, and work your students through a rotation so each one gets a chance to play it and reinforce what he or she has learned throughout the week.

ABC3 Science
http://www.abc.net.au/abc3/science

Kids will love this fun site produced in Australia. Your students can check out science blogs written by the "Surfing Scientist," read articles about current events in science, and play interactive games.

All Science Fair Projects
http://www.all-science-fair-projects.com

From plants to X-ray machines, from elementary to high school, you can find a science fair project that will suit just about any student at any age. Whether you are actually requiring your students to do a science fair project, or you just want to adapt one as a classroom demonstration or experiment, you'll find a lot of cool ideas on this site.

Andrew Lost Classroom Club
http://www.randomhouse.com/teachers/andrewlost

Here's another fun classroom club from Random House Books. This science club is based on the popular Andrew Lost book series by J. C. Greenburg. You'll find teacher guides, links to the books, an e-mail newsletter, and a featured experiment.

Animal Diversity Web
http://animaldiversity.ummz.umich.edu/site/index.html

This is one of my favorite places on the web to start animal research. It is hosted and kept up by the University of Michigan Museum of Zoology and contains information and photographs about most animals

SCIENCE RESOURCES

in the world. If your students need to do animal reports or research, bookmark this site for them.

Arbor Day Foundation
http://www.arborday.org/index.cfm

The Arbor Day Foundation offers many resources on its site to help teachers encourage their students to be stewards of our planet. You'll have to navigate the site a bit to familiarize yourself with where different offers are located, but here you'll find student brochures you can order to raise awareness for Arbor Day and the foundation. You'll also find membership benefits such as a gift of 10 flowering trees appropriate to your planting zone when you become a member for $10 a year.

Ask-A-Geologist
http://walrus.wr.usgs.gov/ask-a-geologist

The U.S. Geological Survey hosts this cool site. If you or your students have a question about volcanoes, earthquakes, mountains, rocks, maps, lakes, and so on, check the FAQ section first, then e-mail it in. Within a few days, your question will be answered graciously by a working geologist.

Ask An Astrophysicist
http://imagine.gsfc.nasa.gov/docs/ask_
astro/ask_an_astronomer.html

Once you check the website thoroughly and still can't find an answer to your students' questions about black holes, dark matter, galaxies, or other space-related topics or technologies, send your question in and an astrophysicist will answer you back.

Astronomy Picture of the Day
http://apod.nasa.gov/apod/astropix.html

This is an incredible website powered by NASA. Each day it features a full-screen photograph with a description beneath it. There is an archive available to search for past pictures.

The Atoms Family
http://www.miamisci.org/af/sln/index.html

This is a fun resource based on The Atoms Family exhibit at the Miami Museum of Science. Here students can learn about energy conservation, the difference between kinetic and potential energy, the principles of atoms and matter, the properties of light, the law of conservation of energy, and more. Resources are first arranged by topic, and then divided by grade level. There are lots of fun, easy, and economical experiments you can try with your students using everyday items.

BBC Schools
http://www.bbc.co.uk/schools/websites/4_11/site/science.shtml

The BBC provides a collection of lessons and games for various subjects. At this link, you'll find loads of interactive games that teach science. Remember that this is a British website, though, and preview each game before allowing your students to play it. Some British word usages may be different than American usages.

SCIENCE RESOURCES

Bill Nye the Science Guy
http://www.billnye.com/for-kids-teachers

How can anyone teach elementary science without showing at least one Bill Nye video? This guy is quirky, nerdy, silly, and fun for kids of all ages. His site is a wonderful mix of real-life science he runs across and chronicles on his blog, demos for you to try in the classroom or for kids to try at home, and guides to using his videos with kids.

BrainPOP
http://www.brainpop.com/science

BrainPOP was created in 1999 by an immunologist to deliver tough information to his young patients in a creative, engaging, nonthreatening way. It now contains hundreds of short, standards-based animations on a variety of curriculum topics and can be used to introduce or supplement various units. Note that it is a subscription-based site, but it offers several videos in each subject area for free. This link will take you to the science video page.

Bubbles
http://www.exploratorium.edu/ronh/bubbles/bubbles.html

This is an Exploratorium site that explains the forces that make bubbles, formulas for making your own bubbles, and links to additional bubble resources.

Bureau of Ocean Energy Management, Regulation, and Enforcement Kids' Page
http://www.boemre.gov/mmskids

The Bureau of Ocean Energy Management, Regulation and Enforcement is a division of the Department of the Interior. This website helps kids understand about off-shore drilling and energy resources, as well as the responsible way energy should be used and collected. There are great interactive games and simulations on this site.

Carefresh Lesson in a Box Small Animal Pet Care Classroom Kit
http://www.petco.com/product/112341/Carefresh-Lesson-In-A-Box-Small-Animal-Pet-Care-Classroom-Kit.aspx

If you are thinking about getting a small animal like a hamster, gerbil, guinea pig, or mouse as a class pet, order this teaching kit from Petco and Carefresh. Each kit contains what you need to teach small animal care to 30 students, and teachers can order one kit each year. The kit consists of lesson plans about small animal pet care, coupons to help offset the cost of classroom pet ownership, coupons for free bedding and food, a DVD, and a pet care poster with stickers.

Charts and Posters
http://thinkzone.wlonk.com/Posters/Posters.htm

Download free math and science posters in PDF format at this site. The posters can print at regular letter size, or the file can be brought to a copy shop that makes poster-sized copies, and you can print them there. Too much of a bother? The site does offer posters for sale, too.

SCIENCE RESOURCES

Coastal Wetlands Planning, Protection, and Restoration Act
http://lacoast.gov/new/Ed/Cds.aspx

This site contains free videos, computer games, brochures, and posters about Louisiana coastal restoration. Some are available for download; others must be sent for.

Cool Science
http://www.hhmi.org/coolscience

This site, presented by the Howard Hughes Medical Institute, has so many resources for teachers and their students that it is impossible to share them all. You need to check out the beautiful site for yourself. The "For Curious Kids" link takes your students on location to meet the dust (and other stuff) in the air, shows them the connection between butterflies and caterpillars, and more. The teacher resource section contains animations, online books, activities, videos, kits, lesson plans, and much more.

Cosmic Quest
http://www.childrensmuseum.org/cosmicquest/index.html

Powered by the SpaceQuest Planetarium at the Indianapolis Children's Museum, Cosmic Quest is an interactive website about the solar system. There is a clickable field guide that gives students quick facts about each planet and the sun, famous astronomers, and spacecraft. There's also an interactive game called "Living in Space."

SCIENCE RESOURCES

Cow's Eye Dissection

http://www.exploratorium.edu/learning_
studio/cow_eye/step01.html

This site is definitely not for the faint of stomach! But it's so cool! And, it's a great way to teach basic anatomy or information about the sense of sight without having to do an actual dissection. Upper elementary kids will love this site.

Deep Earth Academy Resources

http://www.oceanleadership.org/education/
deep-earth-academy/i-dea-resources

There is a disclaimer on the site stating that they may only be able to honor part of your resource request or that it may take extra time to receive your materials, so plan accordingly and order only what you will actively use in your classroom. The Deep Earth Academy presents programs and resources for educators teaching about ocean drilling. Here you'll find posters, stickers with a sticker book, lab books, measuring tapes to help compare ratios, bookmarks, models, pencils, DVDs, and teaching guides.

Dinosaurs for Kids

http://www.kidsdinos.com

Dino lovers in your classroom will love these engaging games and activities designed to help them learn all they can about dinosaurs and the eras in which they lived.

SCIENCE
RESOURCES

Discover Engineering
http://www.discoverengineering.org

Try engineering games and activities, watch videos, meet a skateboard legend, design a roller coaster, learn trivia, and do much more at this site. This cool site will get young kids interested in engineering and help them see that they can do anything they dream.

eNature
http://www.enature.com/home

Search online field guides for information about more than 5,500 different species of plants and animals. Your students can also play games and ask an expert their burning nature questions.

The Earth Life Web
http://www.earthlife.net/begin.html

The Earth Life Web is an index of descriptions about all life on Earth. The author states in his introduction that it will always be under construction, as he is constantly writing, researching, and learning about different forms of life on Earth.

EarthSky
http://earthsky.org

This is the site for a daily science radio program that features subjects that affect our lives like earth science, astronomy, and environmental science. There are news stories and photographs, as well as archived broadcasts.

Endangered Species
http://eelink.net/EndSpp

This is a clearinghouse for all things relating to endangered species. The page contains tons of links to resources of every kind so that you can learn everything you need to know before you begin your class's study on this topic.

Endangered Species Coloring Book: "Save Our Species"
http://www.epa.gov/espp/coloring

If you go to the web link, you'll be able to download the PDF version of this cool coloring book. If you'd like a free hard copy, call or fax (on school stationary) your request for either the coloring book, the poster, or both by using the instructions on the site. You may only be able to receive one copy of each, but you can try asking for a class set of coloring books.

Energy Kids
http://www.eia.gov/kids

The U.S. Energy Information Administration shares this website, chock-full of resources for kids and teachers. Topics include "What Is Energy?," "Energy Sources," "Using and Saving Energy," "History of Energy," and "Games and Activities." For teachers, there is a special section including energy calculators and a glossary.

SCIENCE RESOURCES

EPA Student Center
http://www.epa.gov/students

The Environmental Protection Agency's Student Center includes games, videos, and quizzes. Also available are resources and links about air, climate change, conservation, ecosystems, environmental basics, human heath, waste and recycling, and water. Kids learn how to get involved in conservation projects at the local, state, and national levels.

ES2000: Endangered Species of the Next Millennium
http://library.thinkquest.org/25014/english.index.shtml

You will find plenty of resources for your next unit about endangered species here. This site explains what endangered species are and why they are threatened, and forecasts certain species' life expectancy for the future. It also contains information about what can be done to help.

Exploratorium
http://www.exploratorium.edu/explore

Are you looking for fun, engaging, hands-on activities to breathe new life into your science curriculum? This site has hundreds of suggestions and step-by-step instructions for you.

Exploring Planets in the Classroom
http://www.spacegrant.hawaii.edu/class_acts/index.html

What began as a workshop in Planetary Geosciences at the University of Hawaii at Manoa for K–12 educators has expanded to a website that assists educators from around the world in finding hands-on activi-

SCIENCE RESOURCES

ties to teach elementary, middle, high school, and college students. You'll find both teacher and student pages for all grades on topics such as volcanology, introduction to the solar system, gravity forces, and rockets.

Eye Facts for Children Poster
http://catalog.nei.nih.gov/p-328-eye-facts-for-children-poster.aspx

This fun poster has facts, tips, and myth busters about human and animal eyes. It is provided either as a download or by mail. Both the download and the paper copy are free from the National Eye Institute. The site also offers activity booklets on eyesight and eye care and other items for free, with multiple copies for a small fee.

Free Energy Education Materials
http://www.nef1.org/ngfm.html

Sign up to receive a teaching packet from the National Energy Foundation. The K–3 packet includes a Think! Energy Poster, teacher's guide, CD, safety poster, energy assessment, and classroom set of Think! Energy light switch stickers. The 4–6 packet includes all of the above as well as a newsletter and additional poster.

Free Science Games
http://www.softschools.com/science

Softschools.com provides simple games, activities, and worksheets to challenge elementary students. The science section can be further divided into grade levels.

Free TeachKind Materials for Educators
http://www.teachkind.org/merchandise.asp

The Share the World curriculum is designed to help students appreciate the animals that live in our world. It is designed for students in grades 3–5 and includes a video and printables. There are other resources available that teachers can request here, too.

Frogs
http://www.exploratorium.edu/frogs/index.html

What elementary school kid is not fascinated by amphibians? At this Exploratorium site, you'll find activities, stories, online exhibits, and more about these fun, freaky little creatures.

Fun Science Resources Especially for Students
http://www.reachoutmichigan.org/resources.html

This amazingly comprehensive web guide provides links to many science topics of interest to elementary school students. You have to check this site out to believe it, but make sure you give yourself some time. There are tons of sites linked here to explore.

Geo-Mysteries
http://www.childrensmuseum.org/geomysteries/index2.html

The Children's Museum of Indianapolis provides this cool site to help kids learn more about the makeup and structures of the Earth. There are mysteries to solve, fossil FAQs answered, and tips for kids "going out into the field" to search for rocks and fossils, including how to keep a simple field journal.

Geology.com
http://geology.com

Natural gas prices nationwide, mountains of the moon, "What Does a Geologist Do?," and metamorphic rocks are just a sampling of the categories and topics you and your students can learn about at this site. There are maps available, as well as a store for you to purchase things if you wish.

George Washington Carver Coloring and Activity Book
http://www.dm.usda.gov/oo/colorbook.htm

The U.S. Department of Agriculture offers this printable, activity-packed coloring book biography of George Washington Carver. If you haven't had a chance to share this man's life and work with your students, you should try. He was much more than just a scientist involved in peanut plants.

The Great Plant Escape
http://urbanext.illinois.edu/gpe/gpe.html

This is a fun way to teach about the science of plants—kids get to take on the persona of detectives and solve cases involving plants. They read case files, study (and learn!) the parts of plants, and solve several cases along the way. There is a teacher's guide available to help you make the most of this engaging resource.

SCIENCE
RESOURCES

Human Anatomy Model
http://www.innerbody.com/htm/body.html

For those educators who need to teach units about the body systems, this is a good resource to use with a computer projector or SMART board. Each of the body systems is detailed, with all parts explained and illustrated. You click on a specific system, like the respiratory, skeletal, or muscular system, and an anatomically correct model comes up. You may not want to let kids loose on the site, however, as the reproductive systems are included and some parents may not find that appropriate for their little ones to be checking out just yet. If you use this as a projectable model and pull up the specific system you need to teach on your own computer or SMART board, though, this is a fabulous resource.

Instructables
http://www.instructables.com/index

This is crafting and science all rolled together! You can find directions here for making a simple reading lamp (studying electrical circuits?), a box kite (aerodynamics?), and much more.

Journey North
http://www.learner.org/jnorth

Track the spring as it heads north! This site allows you and your students to track animals as they migrate from warm southern locations to the northern parts of our country each year. The teacher section includes lesson plans, student worksheets, graphic organizers, high-resolution photos of animals, and more. In the fall, the site switches to allow kids to track animals' migrations south.

Kidipede: Science for Kids
http://www.historyforkids.org/scienceforkids/index.htm

This is a fabulous compilation of interactive topics, experiments, teacher's guides, and suggested science fair topics. The site covers biology, physics, chemistry, and geology.

Kids Kreate
http://kidskreate.com

You can find tons of educational craft ideas at this site, including edible artwork, recipes for crafting and art equipment, crafts organized by subject, and much more!

KidsGardening
http://www.kidsgardening.org

The folks at the National Gardening Association believe that, through gardening, adults can enhance all aspects of a kid's growth—educational, social, emotional, and physical. To encourage this, they created this website that features resources, lesson plans, project ideas, and more. You can look through the site to see how gardening can grow from an interesting science project to something that brings the school and community together. They do offer some items for purchase, and you can request a free catalog on this site as well.

The Kids' Science Challenge
http://www.kidsciencechallenge.com/#/home

This site challenges kids to come up with unique science experiments and problems using a set collection of materials, and then sub-

SCIENCE
RESOURCES

mit them for real scientists to solve. The site/challenge sponsors put together an impressive collection of prizes for kids to win. Check back often—the new science kit and challenge is usually only open to the first 1,000 teachers who register, and they go fast. Past challenges have been issued in October.

Koko's Kids Club

http://www.koko.org/kidsclub/teachers

The site is fun and interactive, and your students will love exploring facts and pictures about Koko the gorilla. The teacher's section provides you with two unique opportunities. You can apply to develop curriculum for the site and receive teaching credit from California State University, Monterey Bay, or you can request a link to online resources to teach your students about gorillas and conservation.

LessonPlansPage.com

http://www.lessonplanspage.com/Science.htm

First, choose your grade level, then choose from one of the dozens of great lesson plans on just about any science topic imaginable. The work has been done for you; you just need to plug these creative and fun lessons into your curriculum.

Life Along a Prairie River Poster

http://www.biosurvey.ou.edu/posters/posterorder.html

Order your free full-color (and beautiful) Life Along a Prairie River poster at this site. The posters are free for teachers in Oklahoma, but others can request posters if they pay shipping fees.

SCIENCE RESOURCES

Life of the Forest: Teacher Packet
http://signetstore.com

Order the Life of the Forest Teacher Packet by filling out the online order form. You'll receive a set of posters and handouts about forests including topics such as understanding tree rings, identifying leaves, differentiating trees by their bark, and more. There is also a link to a curriculum you could use to teach these topics.

The Magic School Bus
http://www.scholastic.com/magicschoolbus/games/index.htm

What elementary science program would be complete without some help from Ms. Frizzle? On this website, students can play games that complement episodes, complete activities, and learn more about the books. You can download classroom activities, use your projector or interactive whiteboard to take virtual field trips with Ms. Frizzle, or show episodes of the television show.

Marine Life Poster
http://www.ocol-clo.gc.ca/html/poster_affiche_e.php

The Office of the Commissioner of Official Languages offers several posters for free at this web address. The most applicable to an elementary classroom is the Marine Life poster showcasing several species of ocean animals.

SCIENCE RESOURCES

Mars for Educators
http://mars.jpl.nasa.gov/participate/marsforeducators

Arizona State University and the Jet Propulsion Laboratory partnered to bring you this rich resource full of activities, downloads, tools, and lesson plans for teaching your students about Mars. Additionally, there are links to other projects you can sign up to be a part of.

Mineral Information Institute Teacher Packets
http://www.mii.org/teacherhelpers.html

On this site, you can download several free lessons including "A Study of Earth." You can also opt to order accompanying posters to aid in your teaching for as little as $2.

Minnesota Sea Grant Featured Publications
http://www.seagrant.umn.edu/publications

Help your students learn about invasive species, aquaculture, coastal communities, and more with these free printed resources. Look carefully when you order; some resources are not free and require small fees.

Mr. Nussbaum Science
http://www.mrnussbaum.com/zoocode.htm

Originally started as a class website, Mr. Nussbaum's site has grown to thousands of pages. He creates crazy, unique, and fun games for kids, and is passionate about making learning fun. All of the games on the website are free, but he does sell his games as apps through iTunes, as well.

SCIENCE RESOURCES

NASA: Find Teaching Materials

http://search.nasa.gov/search/edFilterSearch.jsp?empty=true

This page allows you to search by grade, subject, and resource type to see what NASA has available to help you teach your next science unit.

NASA Kids' Club

http://www.nasa.gov/audience/forkids/kidsclub/flash/index.html

Your littlest students can visit NASA with Elmo while bigger kids play games like "Space Lunch." The site includes Internet safety tips for parents and educators and explains to kids how they can protect their online identities.

NASA's Imagine the Universe! Request Form

http://imagine.gsfc.nasa.gov/cgi-bin/pre_order.pl

The Imagine the Universe CD contains the information from several of NASA's websites. There are also posters, booklets, and other resources available free to educators at this site.

National Coalition for Aviation Education Teaching Resources

http://www.aviationeducation.org/html/
teachingresources/teachingresources.htm

The pages here spotlight several locations where teachers can find aviation materials for their classroom. Because most are offered by third-party companies, make sure you check a resource out completely and read all of the fine print. Some require purchases.

SCIENCE RESOURCES

National Geographic Daily News

http://news.nationalgeographic.com/news

Here you'll find a daily posting of social studies, geography, and science news from around the world.

National Geographic Kids

http://kids.nationalgeographic.com/kids

This is an animal lover's dream! There are videos, games, and fun facts for kids to watch, play, and learn about weird, cool, and fun animals from around the world.

National Wildlife Federation Kids

http://www.nwf.org/Kids.aspx

The mission of the National Wildlife Federation is "to inspire Americans to protect wildlife for our children's future." On this portion of its website, you'll find games for your students to play in the classroom and at home, ideas for getting kids outside and interacting with nature, free craft projects, and more. There's a newsletter you can sign up for to receive free projects right in your inbox. The NWF also publishes three magazines: *Wild Animal Baby* is for kids ages 2–4, *Your Big Backyard* is for ages 4–7, and *Ranger Rick* is for ages 7–14. When you click on the titles of individual magazines, you'll see a tab appear on the left side of the page entitled "Parents and Educators." Under this tab you'll see resources like teacher's guides, tips for using the magazine with kids, ideas for how to talk to kids about environmental disasters like oil spills, and more. There are also sample eBook versions of the magazine to flip through as you familiarize yourself with their vision.

SCIENCE RESOURCES

Ology
http://www.amnh.org/ology/index.php

On this fun site from the American Museum of Natural History, you and your students can learn all about different "ologies" like anthropology and archaeology.

Our Restless Earth
http://library.thinkquest.org/4327

Take a look at the material offered here before sharing it with your students, because it's "written for students by students" and so materials on this site should always be vetted first. It is a nice little tutorial in easy-to-understand language and graphics about the restlessness of Earth—plate tectonics.

PBSKids Zoboomafoo
http://pbskids.org/zoboo

Zoboomafoo is a fun animal show produced by the folks at PBS. This link takes you straight to the PBSKids web address for animal science games based on the show.

Pete's PowerPoint Station
http://science.pppst.com/index.html
http://plants.pppst.com/index.html
http://animals.pppst.com/index.html

Bursting with colorful graphics and tons of additional links, this is a website to return to again and again. PowerPoint presentations on just about every subject or topic taught to elementary students can be found at this site, along with bonus sections including free clipart and templates so you can create your own PowerPoints. If you have a projector or interactive whiteboard, this is a great site to go to when introducing a new topic of study.

Physics Central Free Posters
http://www.physicscentral.com/explore/posters.cfm

Can you really warm up a cup of coffee by yelling at it? Believe it or not, you can . . . it would just take a really long time. The set of posters available for download or order here are designed with high school physics students in mind, but I think they would be incredible to display in a gifted resource room or a classroom with bright kids who enjoy seemingly impossible questions.

Physics Poster
http://www.physicsmatters.org/poster.html

This is a really cool poster of Albert Einstein and is available by clicking the e-mail link on the site and requesting that a copy be mailed to you. It's also available as a pdf download.

Planet Protectors' Club
http://www.epa.gov/epawaste/education/kids/ppcform.htm

Declare your classroom full of "Planet Protectors" and receive this kit from the EPA. Only one kit is allowed per classroom, so your students will have to share, but you can encourage them to go to the site at home with their parents, because one is allowed per household, too.

Reeko's Mad Scientist Lab
http://www.reekoscience.com

This site offers projects in science for parents, teachers, and kids. And boy, does it deliver! You and your students can start by building a real volcano, then progress to creating optical illusions and making water flow uphill.

SCI4KIDS
http://www.ars.usda.gov/is/kids

The Agricultural Research Service provides this cool resource for kids. They can check out the "Science Spotlight," where they can learn about a current topic of interest to agricultural scientists. When I checked this resource out last, a slide presentation comparing the game "Space Invaders" to agricultural scientists' fight with invasive species was available. Content changes regularly. There is also a "Science Projects" link, a "Teacher's Desk" tab, and a "Cool Careers" link available to kids.

SCIENCE RESOURCES

Science and Technology World War II Poster
http://www.ww2sci-tech.org/poster/poster.php

By filling out the online order form, you can receive this cool poster depicting technological advancements that were made during World War II. This is probably most appropriate for gifted students or upper elementary to middle school students. It's included because many gifted kids are intensely interested in science, technology, and wars, and this would be a valuable resource for a teacher of these kids to have to pull out. Think about its appropriateness for your classroom before ordering.

The Science of Sound
http://www.galaxy.net/~k12/sound

This is a simple website that includes links to experiments and projects about sound that were designed for use in a second-grade classroom.

Science Monster
http://www.sciencemonster.com

Science Monster has some really bright, fun games and lessons about different areas of elementary science. It was created by the author of the Cool Math websites.

Science Rock
http://schoolhouserock.tv/Science.html

The Schoolhouse Rock science videos are collected here, along with the lyrics to each. There are clickable links to view the videos on You-Tube so you can share them with your students as you introduce new topics in science.

Science Teaching Experiments
http://www.charlesedisonfund.org/
Experiments/experiments.html

Originally offered only by mail as a teaching kit in a sturdy three-ring binder, this is now offered as either a digital download or a binder hard copy for the cost of shipping. Go to the site, where you can read through the table of contents and decide if it is for you. There are eight teaching units containing more than 80 experiments that highlight some of Thomas Alva Edison's greatest work. There is also an incentive program you can join by evaluating the experiments you try with your students. For the time it takes you to fill out the questionnaire, you can receive certificates of achievement for each of your students and a T-shirt and hat for your top-performing student.

Science With Me
http://www.sciencewithme.com

This is a great site that contains songs, videos, coloring sheets, and worksheets for all sorts of science topics. You must become a member to access the resources, but membership is free.

Smokey Kids
http://www.smokeybear.com/kids/?js=1

The Smokey the Bear Kids page teaches students all about how they can band together and work to prevent wildfires. Your students can try activities, play games, and find facts and other information.

Star Child: A Learning Center for Young Astronomers
http://starchild.gsfc.nasa.gov/docs/StarChild

Sponsored by NASA, Star Child is fabulous for everyone! There are tons of games, resources, and lesson plans available to teach and learn about space.

SunWise Program Tool Kit
http://www.epa.gov/sunwise/becoming.html

The Environmental Protection Agency has put together a wonderful kit to help you teach sun safety. You must have a thought-out plan for

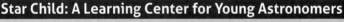

using the materials, and be prepared to fill out a 3-page online appli-cation. It's a really cool kit, though—well worth the effort if you have an idea or need to teach sun safety.

Teachnet.com
http://teachnet.com/category/lessonplans/science

The mission of Teachnet.com is simple: to connect teachers and give them a voice. At this link, you'll find Teachnet.com's science activities. These are quick lessons, games, or tasks that can jump start your les-sons, beef them up, add a hands-on component to a topic you're pre-senting, or just give the kids a break from worksheets.

United Stated Fish and Wildlife Services Management Offices
http://www.fws.gov/offices/statelinks.html

The USFWS is a great starting point when you or your students want to learn about animals in your state. Most state departments offer free, state-specific magazine subscriptions (here in Ohio we receive *Wild Ohio*) and will give you posters and small field guide brochures, and may even come in and talk to your students for free. If you regularly study any animals in your state, get to know your county's wildlife offi-cer. This site contains links to each individual state's department.

USDA Forest Service Resources for Teachers, Kids, and Planners
http://www.fs.fed.us/outdoors/naturewatch/resources.htm

This section of the Forest Service website discusses the Nature Watch program and how you and your students can become involved. It offers photo libraries, live video cams, educational program information, and additional resources for teachers and kids. You can download how-to

SCIENCE RESOURCES

guides for creating vernal pools and other habitats, bat information, and education boxes.

USGS Science Resources for Primary Grades (K–6)
http://education.usgs.gov/common/primary.htm

This page contains links to information, printables, and lesson plans about all areas of science. It is an extremely valuable page that can enrich any science topic you teach—from building your own background knowledge to engaging students in meaningful activities, experiments, and demonstrations.

Using Live Insects in Elementary Classrooms
http://insected.arl.arizona.edu/uli.htm

The University of Arizona Center for Insect Science Outreach offers this site full of lesson plans, information sheets, rearing guides, bibliographies, and standards match-ups.

Water Education Posters
http://water.usgs.gov/outreach/OutReach.html

The U.S. Geological Survey offers bright, engaging posters for each of the different water ecosystems kids study in school. You can download the poster and print it in a small format or take the file on a jump drive to a copy shop where they can print it in a large size for you.

SCIENCE RESOURCES

WaterKids

http://water.epa.gov/learn/kids/waterkids/kids.cfm

Check out WaterKids from the Environmental Protection Agency. Under the "Education & Training" tab, you'll find dozens of lessons and projects all related to water. The "Kids" tab gives you links to water information that is appropriate for kids to check out themselves.

Web Weather for Kids

http://eo.ucar.edu/webweather

The University Corporation for Atmospheric Research (UCAR) provides this site full of information, games, and interactive quizzes for elementary students.

Weekly Online Lessons

http://www.learnersonline.com/weekly/subject/science.htm
http://www.learnersonline.com/weekly/subject/tech.htm

The weekly online lesson archive is just one example of Learners Online's commitment to helping teachers and families find online materials. Each week, it presents science topics based on current events and highlights links to further resources.

Western Regional Air Partnership

http://www.wrapair.org/kids/index.html

WRAP offers a full-color, downloadable student handout about air pollution and conservation.

SCIENCE RESOURCES

The Yuckiest Site on the Internet
http://yucky.discovery.com/flash

Okay . . . quick disclaimer, here: This is one of my favorite sites for kids! Leave it to Discovery Education to find a way to make learning about roaches, worms, or the human body so gross it's cool. Here you'll find "yucky fun & games," "roach world," "worm world," and "your gross and cool body." Kids will be so entertained they won't even realize that they're learning anatomy and physiology. When I taught third grade, I used this site as a literacy center to engage some of my reluctant boy readers. I printed an "Internet Scavenger Hunt" that I made up with simple questions they could answer and tasks they could complete simply by reading the gross material on the site. It was my most popular literacy center—and the cheapest to pull together!

SCIENCE
RESOURCES

Frugal Fun
Activities and Resources to Promote Science Without Spending Money

Engineering Area

Science is all about figuring things out. I once visited a science center with my kids. One of our favorite exhibits was simply a room filled with old, broken electronics. There were tool belts for kids to wear, complete with kid-sized tools. We all went to town, taking things apart and trying to fit them back together or build new things. One of the most important science skills to teach is flexibility. Scientists need to think flexibly about what is known and unknown. They need to be brave enough to try to solve an unsolvable problem. Let your students try, too.

- Ask parents to send in broken or no-longer-working electronics, and let your students take them apart to see how all of the parts work together.
- Set out building supplies like blocks, manipulatives, K'nex, and LEGOs, and give your students time for free explorations.
- Set up an open-ended building challenge (like a box of craft sticks and glue). See what your students come up with. Do they design a building? A person?

Forces and Motion

Old toy cars, a 2x4 from your neighbor's backyard, and a stack of books is all you need to teach kids about gravity, force, motion, and incline. Add some weight to the car for resistance (tape on some pennies). How about throwing a friction study in there? Do you have an old towel or carpet remnant you can clip to the board? Or a bunch of rubber bands to wrap around it? There are a lot of science kits on the market that teachers often buy to help their students learn about this kind of science. Remember to think about what you already own. You may be able to come up with some great science experiments or demonstrations with things like these.

How Can You Lift Your Teacher?

Start out a unit on simple machines with this fun challenge. Ask your students if anyone can lift you. Let a few of the strongest try, and then teach them how to make a simple lever with a board and brick. Now have one of your smallest kids lift you with the lever. This powerful demonstration doesn't take any money. Ask for a board and brick from a construction site or somewhere else.

Leaf Rubbings

This is an old standby lesson for a reason. Little ones are fascinated by the textures that crayons bring out when leaf rubbings are made. The nature walk to collect the leaves is just as exciting to kids as the rubbings themselves. Older kids can label their rubbings with the type of leaf or the parts of a leaf.

Nature Study

Textbooks, movies, the media, and everyone else talks about the problems facing Earth, and how we can protect its future. I think the best way to teach kids about protecting Earth and its resources is to teach them to love it.

o Take them for walks outside. You don't have to be in a suburb or rural area to see trees, grass, birds, squirrels, and other signs of nature.

o Bring nature to them. Stop by a pond or stream and scoop out a plastic aquarium or container of water. You're likely to get many different organisms and other treasures. Show students what the water looks like under the microscope after they've had a chance to observe the obvious. They'll be amazed at the number of microorganisms they'll see.

o Decorate the classroom with flowers, plants, pretty rocks, and shells.

o Plan sensory areas with leaves, twigs, acorns, and other things from outside.

o Create art with found objects from nature walks.

Observation Stations

Set up some windowsill science in your classroom. Give students time to explore the materials and use their inquiry skills and senses to observe and record what they see. Use inexpensive or free materials that you've asked parents, friends, or local businesses to send in.

o **Birding:** Set out children's binoculars, bird identification guides, journal or notebook pages, colored pencils and other drawing or writing equipment, and a kid-friendly camera or video camera. Outside, place bird feeders, nectar sippers, and birdbaths.

o **Plants:** Offer students a bucket of soil, small cups, seeds, plant journals (paper folded into small books and stapled), magnifying glasses, and a microscope (if available).

o **Small Worlds:** Set out micro viewers, microscopes, magnifying glasses, and small things to look at (e.g., seeds, pollen, petals, leaves, nuts, hair, prepared slides, buttons), and science journals.

o **Float or Sink:** Have a tub of water, small objects, and recording paper (and towels!).

Paper Airplane Play

Science doesn't have to be complicated—in fact, it should be fun. Teach your students that science is everywhere by playing around a little. Show them how to make a simple paper airplane. Demonstrate how it flies, and have them try theirs out. Then, ask your students to think about how they could make them better. Have them *experiment* by trying different weights of paper and different folds, and just playing around. Afterward, you can mention aerodynamics in an age-appropriate way (e.g., the air moves . . .).

Seasons of a Tree

Observations can give primary students great insight into weather, change, and nature. Choose a tree to "adopt" as a class, and once each season, visit the tree with clipboards, paper, pencils, and colored pencils to record its appearance. Older students can add anecdotal observations about the different plants and animals that are around during each season or any other observations that fit within your curriculum goals.

CHAPTER 6

Social Studies Resources

Like science, social studies is becoming a long-lost subject in elementary classrooms across the country. Social studies is a broad descriptor that covers topics such as history, geography, economics, government, citizenship, and culture. Students learn that they are part of a community and that their community is part of a larger world. Elementary students begin to have an awareness of the larger picture of the world.

Social studies education lays a foundation and teaches kids what they need to know in order to grow to be active adults engaged in preserving democracy and civic liberties in our country. They learn why we celebrate national holidays, who some of our country's founders are, and how we tie in to the rest of the world. Elementary kids also learn about the people who make their own communities safe places to be, how laws are made, and how they can be changed.

A solid foundation in the social studies can help shape kids. Even if you are in a district that doesn't have a formal social studies curriculum, or your time to spend on this subject is being cut, like so many, down to an hour or less each week, try to incorporate it into other subject areas. Just like science, social studies is easy to sneak into reading and writing lessons.

When you need to teach your students how to read for meaning, have them read one of the many wonderful children's biographies available today. Have them write a story about someone who lived during pioneer times after listening to you read aloud from *Little House on the Prairie*. Set up an exploration center that contains copies of historical documents, and challenge them to write their own classroom laws in the flowery language of our forefathers.

If you need a little inspiration or some free resources to help you bring social studies alive for your students, or if you need new ways to integrate it into other subject areas, you're sure to find what you need in this chapter. There are posters and pencils, games and puzzles, and lesson plans that you can download. Cross-curricular themes have already been put together for you; all you need to do is incorporate them into your lesson plan book and find some books at your school or public library.

Bookmark some of your favorite games on the computer, and let your students play away as they learn map skills, match up the states and their capitals, discover what imports and exports are, and much more. This chapter can easily kick your social studies curriculum from barely there to integrated across curricular areas and throughout the week.

50States.com
http://www.50states.com

This site is an online "book" filled with information and fun facts about all of the states and their capitals. There are additional links to state flower information, trivia and puzzles, and much more.

A&E Classroom: Teaching Materials
http://www.aetv.com/class/teachingmaterials

The website of the Arts and Entertainment Television Network is an incredible resource. The network includes A&E, the History Channel, and Biography. The site features complete program information and hundreds of online lesson plans. You can also order a biannual Idea Book to help you plan your lessons.

African American Odyssey
http://memory.loc.gov/ammem/aaohtml/exhibit/aointro.html

The Library of Congress presents this online, illustrated book describing the history of African Americans in our nation. It goes through slavery, the Antebellum period, abolition, the Civil War, Reconstruction, the era of Booker T. Washington, World War I, the Depression, the New Deal, World War II, and Civil Rights. Mostly appropriate for older students, it is a great resource for background information as you plan your lessons for Black History month or to discuss an overview of American history with upper elementary kids.

African Studies Center

http://www.africa.upenn.edu/Home_Page/AFR_GIDE.html

This site can help you find anything you need to introduce your students to the continent of Africa and its countries. Further categorized, you can click on country-specific information, languages, environments, and travel, as well as lesson plans and workshops.

America Rock

http://schoolhouserock.tv/America.html

The Schoolhouse Rock videos are collected here, along with the lyrics to each. There are clickable links to view the videos on YouTube so you can share them with your students as you introduce new topics about the history of our nation.

The American Presidency: A Glorious Burden

http://americanhistory.si.edu/presidency/home.html

This colorful site is presented by the Smithsonian Institute and is about the job of being president. On the teacher materials page, you'll find lesson plans, along with a guide for using the website with your class. You'll also find bibliographies of books about the presidency, presidents, and the White House. There are also pages that host links to additional resources and activities for kids to do.

American Treasures of the Library of Congress

http://www.loc.gov/exhibits/treasures

Here you'll find descriptions of some of the rare and significant items found in the Library of Congress. You can check out online scans of such items as the handwritten draft of the Declaration of Independence and photographs of soldiers during various American wars.

America's Byways Map
http://www.byways.org/map_request.html

At this link, you can order a full-color, poster-sized map of America's byways. The National Scenic Byways program is affiliated with the National Department of Transportation. It is an effort to preserve scenic travel routes throughout the country.

America's Heritage: An Adventure in Liberty
http://www.americanheritage.org/curriculum.html

Do you teach elementary social studies and need to supplement a bit more about American History? This site offers curriculum as a completely free download or requestable CD. If you prefer to have a hard copy, you pay a fee to have a curriculum binder with all of the printouts organized for you.

America's Story From America's Library
http://www.americaslibrary.gov

This is a fun and comprehensive site for kids learning about our country. The Library of Congress encourages kids to "Meet Amazing Americans," "Jump Back in Time," "Explore the States," "Join America at Play," and "See, Hear, and Sing."

AnyDay: Today in History
http://www.scopesys.com/anyday

Find historic events and birthdays associated with any day of the year. This is a great resource for teachers who have calendar time each day or hold class meetings.

Archiving Early America
http://www.earlyamerica.com

This rich, packed website features newspapers, maps, and writings from early America. Find writings from the pages of Thomas Jefferson's journals, portraits and brief biographies of famous Americans, games, music from historic time periods, and online videos to watch.

Asia for Educators
http://afe.easia.columbia.edu

For all levels of students and educators, this resource is an initiative of the Weatherhead East Asian Institute at Columbia University. You'll find information on Asian geography, maps, videos, lesson plans, and puzzles. You'll also find games and recipes.

Asia Society
http://asiasociety.org/education/resources-schools

The Asia Society provides many great resources for teachers who teach about Asia. You will find information about afterschool programs, school resources, and games and pictographs for kids.

AwesomeStories

http://www.awesomestories.com/about-us

The site includes hundreds of links to firsthand stories about people, disasters, trials, and other aspects of history. There are lesson plans available, and the stories themselves are good lesson/topic/unit starters that can help you get your students hooked and make them feel like they are there—a part of history.

BBC History for Kids

http://www.bbc.co.uk/history/forkids

Here, kids can learn about ancient history, world history, British history, England, Northern Ireland, Scotland, and Wales. They can also discover hands-on resources for learning history like building their own castle and making their own cave art.

BBC Schools

http://www.bbc.co.uk/schools/websites/4_11/
site/geography.shtml
http://www.bbc.co.uk/schools/websites/4_11/site/history.shtml

The BBC provides a collection of lessons and games for various subjects. At these links, you'll find loads of interactive games that teach geography and history. Remember that this is a British website, though, and preview each game before allowing your students to play it. Some British word usages may be different than American usages.

SOCIAL STUDIES
RESOURCES

Ben's Guide to U.S. Government for Kids
http://bensguide.gpo.gov

Ben's Guide provides resources for kids, teachers, and parents that teach how our government works. It uses primary source documents and encourages active involvement in our government systems. Users choose a grade level before entering so they are placed in an appropriate section of the site.

Benjamin Franklin: Glimpses of the Man
http://sln.fi.edu/franklin

This is a comprehensive look at the life and work of Benjamin Franklin. Kids will learn some really neat things about his life. For example, did you know that he was an accomplished musician and could predict the weather? Teachers, you'll find links to additional resources to help you develop a unit about this remarkable man.

Best of History Websites
http://besthistorysites.net

You'll find an annotated list of links to hundreds of different history sites here. You'll be directed to lesson plans, teacher guides, activities, games, and quizzes. You can choose from categories such as prehistory, ancient/Biblical, medieval, American, early modern Europe, and World War II. You can also choose based on categories like art, maps, lesson plans, games, and research.

SOCIAL STUDIES
RESOURCES

Biographical Dictionary
http://www.s9.com

The Biographical Dictionary is a Wikipedia-type site that includes biographies about people from history as well as current celebrities. As with Wikipedia, this is a good source to begin your research or find tidbits or cool facts, but then be sure to verify the information with another source or two before taking it as fact. These biographies do not list source materials or citations.

Biography Maker
http://bellinghamschools.org/department-owner/curriculum/biography-maker

The Biography Maker is hosted by the Bellingham Public Schools (Washington) district website. It is a unique, interactive writing program that helps kids write a biography and understand this genre. Kids are inspired to write engaging stories that excite readers and prompt them to try to learn more about the subject of the biography.

Birthday Traditions From Around the World
http://www.kidsparties.com/traditions.htm

As you teach about how kids are the same and different around the world, don't forget to talk about birthday celebrations. This is one topic most kids can relate to, and this site has descriptions about traditions of countries and families from around the world.

A Book in Time
http://www.abookintime.com/index.html

Here you'll find lists of historical fiction and nonfiction, craft ideas related to those books, links to outside websites, and timelines for kids. There is a history reading timeline that is organized in chronological order and lists both world and American history.

BrainPOP
http://www.brainpop.com/socialstudies

BrainPOP was created in 1999 by an immunologist to deliver tough information to his young patients in a creative, engaging, nonthreatening way. It now contains hundreds of short, standards-based animations on a variety of curriculum topics and can be used to introduce or supplement various units. Note that it is a subscription-based site, but it offers several videos in each subject area for free. This link will take you to the social studies video page.

The Civil War for Fifth Graders
http://www.radford.edu/~sbisset/civilwar.htm

This site was created by a fifth-grade teacher to help teach her students about the Civil War. She includes links to a few additional interactive sites, as well as a printable "treasure hunt" to help kids get a deeper understanding of the material presented on this page.

CongressLink

http://www.congresslink.org/print_lp_contents.htm

Do you need to teach your young students about U.S. Government? Check this site out! You'll find lesson plans, webquests, websites, online textbooks, glossaries, historical notes, assessment rubrics, and multimedia views of Capitol Hill.

Countries

http://kids.nationalgeographic.com/kids/places/find

When your students click on a country, they'll be able to view an annotated slideshow of photographs from that location. Once they are on the page related to a specific country, they can choose the tab marked "Video" to learn about the geography of that country in an animated and photographed online video segment. The map tab will take them to a labeled map showing where the country is in the world. Finally, they can send an e-card to a friend or parent and print out a collectible trading card and information about the country.

DIG Cool Links

http://www.digonsite.com/links.html

This is a list of cool archaeology sites for kids and teachers to explore.

Digital History

http://www.digitalhistory.uh.edu

The mission of this site is to help teachers use new technologies to enhance teaching and research. You'll find links to teaching guides, documents, timelines, museum exhibits, videos, and much more.

Discoverers Web
http://www.win.tue.nl/cs/fm/engels/discovery

If you need to teach a unit on explorers, look no further than this site as a place to start gathering materials. There are dozens of links collected here for you about explorers from around the world and throughout history.

DownloadLearning.com
http://www.downloadlearning.com/collections/11

Free award-winning downloadable software programs that teach everything from explorers and scientists to history and geography can be found at this site. These games can enrich any classroom curriculum. And if you need proof of their validity, the site offers a standards match-up page so you can see the standard each title covers.

Dynamo's History
http://www.bbc.co.uk/education/dynamo/history

This site has fun and games—all related to history for young learners. For example, you and your students can find out how people lived 100 years ago. Your students won't even realize that they're learning as they're entertained by the site's animations and music.

edHelper.com
http://www.edhelper.com/Social_Studies.htm

edHelper is a great site—one I've used for years. Many resources are offered for free, like the social studies theme units found on this page for grades 1–6. You can also purchase a yearly subscription for a nomi-

SOCIAL STUDIES RESOURCES

nal fee that allows you access to all of its content, including customiz-able activity sheets. You can find comprehension, puzzle, and activity worksheets on just about any topic, along with lesson plans, recipes, and craft ideas.

EDSITEment! The Best of the Humanities on the Web
http://edsitement.neh.gov/lesson-plans

Powered by the National Endowment for the Humanities, this lesson plans site offers much more than just lesson plans. It's a database that you can search by subject, theme, and grade level. You can find activities and lessons to tie social studies into your literature and lan-guage arts curriculum, and you can find great websites and student resources, too!

Education World
http://www.educationworld.com/a_lesson/archives/soc_sci.shtml

This is a nice compilation of lesson plans, articles, and other resources for teaching social studies to kids of all ages. My favorite lesson is "Using Old Newspapers to Teach History."

Eduweb
http://www.eduweb.com/portfolio/portfolio.php

Eduweb is a developer of online learning games. Browse their site by subject or grade level to find a learning activity that may enhance your social studies lessons.

The FBI Kids Page
http://www.fbi.gov/fun-games/kids/kids

Fun and games abound at this site—all designed to teach kids in grades K–5 about the Federal Bureau of Investigation. Kids can help a special agent find a disguise to help him go undercover, learn about FBI dogs, learn how to keep themselves safe, discover how investigations take place, and even join in on an adventure.

Focus on Your Community
http://community.rice.edu/focusresources

The lesson plans and other resources offered here encourage you to use local history and community studies as a way to give students a holistic sense of the role of history in understanding the world.

The Food Timeline
http://www.foodtimeline.org/food2.html

This is a unique site that indexes loads of resources about the role of food in history. There is a USA Food History guide available that explores native food sources as well as the origins of American classics like apple pie and hot dogs. There are also many links to agricultural history and foods from around the world.

Free Historical Thinking Poster
http://teachinghistory.org/poster-request

Teaching History will send you a free "Historical Thinking" or "Civil War" poster at this link.

SOCIAL STUDIES RESOURCES

Free Social Studies Worksheets and Games
http://www.softschools.com/social_studies

Softschools.com provides simple games, activities, and worksheets to challenge elementary students. The social studies section can be further divided into grade levels.

Games on HISTORY
http://www.history.com/games

From History.com and the History Channel, these games are designed to get kids and adults of all ages involved in learning about history. There are some great resources here, including a "Place the State" game and an "Expedition" game that are applicable to elementary classrooms, but, as the games are also modeled after the different TV shows available on the History Channel, some games may not be appropriate for young learners. Preview each game first, then, when you find one that will complement your lessons, either use it as a class with an interactive whiteboard or projector, or bookmark the game itself, not the History.com site.

Geographia—World Travel Destinations, Culture, and History Guide
http://www.geographia.com

This site shares beautiful photographs and information from countries and cultures around the world and can easily serve as background knowledge for the teacher gathering information or as virtual field trips to share new locations with students.

Geography Games

http://www.sheppardsoftware.com/Geography.htm

The folks at Sheppard Software offer a collection of free geography games for students to play online. You'll find games to enhance any geography curriculum. Categories include Africa, Asia, Canada, the Caribbean, Europe, Mexico, Middle East, Oceania, Central and South America, the United States, and the world.

Geonet

http://www.eduplace.com/geonet

Students can choose a region of the United States, a difficulty level, and a category and test their knowledge of geography with this online game.

Gold Rush!

http://pbskids.org/wayback/goldrush

Kids can follow the journey of prospectors as they attempt to strike it rich in the gold mines. They can "meet" a gold rush expert, find jokes about American history, and learn about people affected by the Gold Rush. Teachers can check out the link for teachers and parents to find out cool ways to use this PBS site with students.

Google Earth Lessons

http://gelessons.com/lessons

You've probably checked out Google Earth at some point. Have you ever wondered how to incorporate that incredible and fun resource into your classroom? This site has compiled tons of ideas for you, from

SOCIAL STUDIES RESOURCES

lesson plans to tutorials, along with pictures and lessons created by students.

Government Resources
http://government.mrdonn.org/index.html

Games, lesson plans, worksheets, and activities for teaching about government in elementary classrooms are included here. You can find topics such as the U.S. government, the Constitution, the three branches of government in the U.S., world governments, and more.

Historic Maps in K–12 Classrooms
http://publications.newberry.org/k12maps

This site was created by the staff of the Hermon Dunlap Smith Center for the History of Cartography at the Newberry Library. It includes standards correlations as well as an index of downloadable maps and corresponding lesson plans.

Internet Geography
http://www.geography.learnontheinternet.co.uk

This is a great, long-running site featuring information and resources to enhance your students' love of geography. There is a teacher's section with links to additional resources as well as interactive games.

Kidipede History and Science for Kids
http://www.historyforkids.org

Find out all about ancient civilizations like Egypt, Greece, Rome, China, Africa, West Asia, India, and more, including medieval Europe and American history. Each section contains lots of links, interactive games, and resources, along with a teacher's guide specific to that portion of history.

Kids Geo

http://www.kidsgeo.com/geography-games/index.php

"Geography Games for Kids, Games About Our Earth" is the motto at this colorful site. Your students can match up countries to their correct places on continent maps, match states and their capitals, and play longitude and latitude games.

Kids Next Door

http://www.hud.gov/kids/index.html

The center for Housing and Urban Development (HUD) teaches kids how to be good neighbors through interactive games, virtual field trips, and interesting, colorful graphics.

Kindness Resources for Educators

http://www.randomactsofkindness.org/Educators

Kindness, compassion, and empathy are all valuable social skills that can be taught within the context of caring for and learning about others. The Random Acts of Kindness Foundation offers an educator's page that includes links to lesson plans, arts and crafts, and service project ideas for you to use in your classroom.

Learning About Lincoln

http://www.abrahamlincoln200.org/learning-about-lincoln/
for-teachers/default.aspx?ekmensel=c580fa7b_14_96_btnlink

Although this site was originally created for the bicentennial celebration of Abraham Lincoln's birth, it still provides free resources to teachers. Here, you can download fact sheets, posters, lesson plans, and more. Try changing up how you teach about Lincoln's birthday each February!

The Library of Congress: Teachers
http://www.loc.gov/teachers

Many great, free resources can be found at the Library of Congress site. Teachers can receive classroom materials, either in downloadable documents or mailed to their classroom, and they can find professional development resources.

The Life of Abraham Lincoln
http://www.berwickacademy.org/lincoln/lincoln.htm

This is a fun example of a kid-created website. The students in the first-grade class at Berwick Academy in Maine created this site in 1997. It includes an illustrated timeline of Abraham Lincoln's life, a gallery, and links for kids to learn more about our 16th president. There is a "Tips for Teachers" link that includes information on how the kids made their site and their resource list for additional reading about Abraham Lincoln. A site like this could serve as a spark that ignites your students' passions about publishing their own work.

The Life of Martin Luther King Jr.
http://golden-legacy.com/mlk/mlkjr1.html

This is an online comic book detailing the life of Dr. Martin Luther King Jr. Print it or share it on an interactive whiteboard or with an LCD projector.

Map Adventures
http://egsc.usgs.gov/isb/pubs/teachers-packets/mapadventures

Originally published as a hard copy activity book, Map Adventures is now available as a PDF on the U.S. Geological Society's website. It teaches basic mapping skills along with how to see things from different perspectives.

Maps.com
http://www.maps.com/FunFacts.aspx?nav=FF#

Loads of map games are available here! Students can check out map games, crossword puzzles, tournaments, and more. You can find a game here to supplement just about any geography topic you need to cover.

Maritime Administration: Just for Kids and Teachers
http://www.marad.dot.gov/education_
landing_page/k_12/kids.htm

This site is presented by the Maritime Administration, a division of the U.S. Department of Transportation. You can use these lessons and activities to teach kids about the merchant marines, get lesson plans from the link that leads to the American Association of Port Authorities, and learn about African American war veterans.

Mayflower History Information for Teachers
http://www.mayflowerhistory.com/Introduction/teachers.php

As there are many myths and misconceptions about the lives of the Pilgrims, author Caleb Johnson prepared this resource page to guide you as you plan your teaching unit. Mayflowerhistory.com includes a biography about every passenger who was aboard the Mayflower, a useful resource for teachers who want to add a little meat to their traditional Thanksgiving study.

Mummies of Ancient Egypt
http://www2.si.umich.edu/chico/mummy

Your students can use this site to learn more about mummies—a topic that fascinates kids of all ages—and gets them interested in learning more about history.

My Wonderful World
http://www.mywonderfulworld.org/index.html

My Wonderful World is a national campaign led by National Geographic with the mission of giving "kids the power of global knowledge." They host a blog with news and notes, promote "Geography Awareness Week," and have games, lessons, and other resources for parents, teachers, and kids of all ages. It's a really well-done program.

National Atlas
http://nationalatlas.gov

The U.S. Geological Survey put together this online, interactive world atlas. Here you'll find a mapmaker, articles, printable maps, and more to enhance your geography lessons.

National Council for the Social Studies Resources
http://www.socialstudies.org/resources

NCSS hosts this resource page containing some of the greatest resources available for teachers. Here you can search through lesson plans, an online Teacher's Library-U.S. History Collection, trade book lists, and helpful and informative articles.

National Geographic Daily News
http://news.nationalgeographic.com/news

Here you'll find a daily posting of social studies, geography, and science news from around the world.

National Geographic Education: Mapping
http://education.nationalgeographic.com/education/mapping

National Geographic Education provides this wonderful site full of mapping resources and activities. At the time of this writing, the site is in Beta form, but promises to add to its value in the future. In Beta, the entire education website is wonderful.

SOCIAL STUDIES
RESOURCES

NationMaster.com
http://www.nationmaster.com/index.php

This site is probably more useful for upper elementary, middle, and high school teachers, but it's so interesting that I wanted to include it anyway. At this site, you can compare two different countries according to various statistical data. For example, did you know that only one book is produced annually in Burma, compared to 347 produced annually in Sri Lanka? Or that Colombia has only seven Subway restaurants compared to the 25 in France? Some of the statistics are a little outdated, but the site still gives a nice comparison of the differences between countries.

NOVA Online: Pyramids—The Inside Story
http://www.pbs.org/wgbh/nova/pyramid

Based on a program aired on NOVA, this PBS site gives you and your students a chance to virtually explore a real pyramid.

The Oregon Trail
http://www.isu.edu/~trinmich/Oregontrail.html

This site was designed for elementary teachers and homeschoolers. You can find great resources here for both you and your students. There is a mini textbook, a map of historical sites along the trail, fantastic (and strange) facts, an archive of diaries and books written about or from the Oregon Trail, and more.

Outreach World

http://www.outreachworld.org/index.asp

Outreach World is a web compilation of resources for teaching kids about the world. When you click the resources tab, you can search for information about specific countries and cultures, and narrow your search by grade level. Although there are mostly resources here for middle and high school teachers, I did find some wonderful K–6 lessons like "Teaching Japan Through Children's Literature" and "Egyptian Paper."

Penn Museum—Educational Resources

http://www.penn.museum/program-resources.html

This is a link to free PDF teacher's guides on topics related to current exhibits and holdings in the museum. Although they are designed to be combined with a visit, the guides themselves are valuable to any teacher preparing a unit on these topics.

Pete's PowerPoint Station

http://socialstudies.pppst.com/index.html
http://occupations.pppst.com/index.html
http://ancienthistory.pppst.com/index.html
http://americanhistory.pppst.com/index.html
http://worldhistory.pppst.com/index.html
http://50states.pppst.com/index.html
http://government.pppst.com/index.html
http://countries.pppst.com/index.html
http://geography.pppst.com/index.html
http://continents.pppst.com/index.html
http://regions.pppst.com/index.html

SOCIAL STUDIES RESOURCES

Bursting with colorful graphics and tons of additional links, this is a website to return to again and again. PowerPoint presentations on just about every subject or topic taught to elementary students can be found at this site, along with bonus sections including free clipart and templates so you can create your own PowerPoints. If you have a projector or interactive whiteboard, this is a great site to go to when introducing a new topic of study.

Postcards From America
http://www.postcardsfrom.com

If you're teaching about United States geography or capital cities, you need to check out this site. A former history teacher and her photographer husband visited all 50 state capitals and created unique postcards to send virtually to website subscribers around the country.

Presidents: The Secret History
http://pbskids.org/wayback/prez/index.html

Kids can learn about the history of presidents. They can find out secrets about presidents and hit the campaign trail with candidates. Teachers can check out the link for teachers and parents to find cool ways to use this PBS site with students.

Quicklinks for Elementary School Teachers
http://teachinghistory.org/quick-links-elementary

Teachinghistory.org is a one-stop resource for teachers who want to understand their subject matter better and come away with easy-to-implement lesson ideas for their curricula.

Smart Fun Online
http://www.hfmgv.org/exhibits/smartfun/index.html

The Henry Ford Museum presents this website showing a road trip taken in a Model T and information about colonial life, as well as teacher resources and links to curriculum content standards.

Smithsonian Education
http://smithsonianeducation.org/index.html

This is the gateway to the Smithsonian's education resources for students, teachers, and families. Here you'll find hundreds of resources, along with websites that take you on tours from your own hometown—wherever that may be—to global locations. Kids can even find homework help on the student pages.

Smithsonian Education: History and Culture
http://www.smithsonianeducation.org/educators/
lesson_plans/history_culture.html

This lesson plan site features printable lesson plans and units about various history and culture topics. You need Adobe Acrobat to view these pages.

Social Studies for Kids
http://www.socialstudiesforkids.com

There are so many great resources on this website, that it was hard to choose which to share. The first thing you need to do when you visit is go to the Teaching Resources page and click on "suggestions

SOCIAL STUDIES
RESOURCES

on using this site." It can be overwhelming. You'll find lesson plans, games, quizzes, and worksheets for kids of all ages.

The Star-Spangled Banenr

http://americanhistory.si.edu/starspangledbanner

This is a Smithsonian Institute site about the flag that inspired our national anthem. You and your students can explore features of the flag, sing along with the anthem, and answer 14 quiz questions to put stars on the flag.

State Facts for Students

http://www.census.gov/schools/facts

Teachers can download the "Picture Your State" lesson plan from the U.S. Census Bureau here, while students can click on various states to find out information about each.

StateMaster.com

http://www.statemaster.com/index.php

This is another great site similar to the NationMaster.com site introduced earlier. Students can select two states and a category to compare, and see how the states match up.

The Story of Africa

http://www.bbc.co.uk/worldservice/africa/features/storyofafrica

Produced by the BBC as a world service, this site feels like an online illustrated book. The pictures are beautiful, a table of contents rides the left margin, and the content of the book takes you and your students through descriptions of events and characters that shaped the continent of Africa and eventually ended apartheid.

Teacher Guide—George Washington: A National Treasure
http://www.georgewashington.si.edu/kids/teacherguide.html

This was once available by mail, but (like many of these resources) is now only accessible as a free download. On this page, you'll find links to the entire teacher's guide and a PDF poster to help you teach students about our nation's first president.

Teaching With Historic Places
http://www.cr.nps.gov/nr/twhp/SSstandards.htm

Although this website contains more than 130 ready-to-use lesson plans on topics and places around the country, its use is not limited to a lesson plan site. When you click on a link about a historic building or other place, you'll find descriptions of the location and photographs. You can easily couple these links with some of the lesson plans and use a projector or interactive whiteboard to take your students on a virtual field trip.

Teachnet.com
http://teachnet.com/category/lessonplans/social-studies/history

The mission of Teachnet.com is simple: to connect teachers and give them a voice. At this link, you'll find Teachnet.com's social studies activities. These are quick lessons, games, or tasks that can jump start your lessons, beef them up, add a hands-on component to a topic you're presenting, or just give the kids a break from worksheets.

SOCIAL STUDIES RESOURCES

United Nations Cyberschoolbus

http://www.un.org/Pubs/CyberSchoolBus/index.shtml

Kids (and teachers!) can learn about human rights, find data about different countries, learn how the UN works, and listen to webcasts of meetings and events. Teachers can browse a list of UN publications—most must be purchased, but occasionally a resource is offered for free.

United States Patent and Trademark Office Kids' Pages

http://www.uspto.gov/web/offices/ac/ahrpa/opa/kids

Encourage your students to use their imaginations and get inventing! On this site, you'll find games and contests, stories, posters, and copyright history. Your students will learn a ton and be inspired to start creating.

The US50

http://www.theus50.com

This site includes information about the 50 states in the United States. You can click on a state on the map for information about that state or visit the links tab to find more resources. Check out the "Backyard USA" section for an account of the state written by someone who actually lives there.

U.S. Census Bureau Kids' Corner

http://factfinder.census.gov/home/en/kids/kids.html

Your students can learn about the census, play games, and take quizzes at this site created by the U.S. Census Bureau.

USGS Science Resources for Primary Grades (K–6)
http://education.usgs.gov/common/primary.htm

Hmmm . . . what is a page about science resources doing in the section on social studies? You'll find the link to this page in science, too, but I thought it was important to include it here as well. If you scroll to the bottom of the page, you'll find links to geography resources—some of them very valuable.

Virtual Antarctica
http://www.doc.ic.ac.uk/~kpt/terraquest/va

Because visiting Antarctica is out of the question for most of us, try a virtual visit when you teach your students about world geography. This site will allow you to show your students firsthand the weather, glaciers, and animals in Antarctica.

Wacky Patent of the Month
http://www.colitz.com/site/wacky_new.html

This is a funny site for you to share with your classroom full of imaginative inventors. Let them know that people are still coming up with inventions, some amazingly necessary and some amazingly bizarre. The last time I checked the site out before sending this book off to my editor, Michael J. Colitz, registered patent attorney and host of the site, shared the story of the bird diaper, designed for pet birds to wear so they could be free to fly around your house. Strange, true, and a fun way to get your students to think outside the box.

Weekly Online Lessons

http://www.learnersonline.com/weekly/subject/ss_hist.htm

http://www.learnersonline.com/weekly/subject/gov.htm

The weekly online lesson archive is just one example of Learners Online's commitment to helping teachers and families find online materials. Each week, it presents social studies and history topics based on current events and highlights links to further resources. Many of the resources are geared toward middle school and high school teachers, but if you look through the archives, you'll likely find gems to use in your classroom as well.

White House 101

http://www.whitehouse.gov/about/white-house-101

Included on the official site of the White House are links to maps, presidential biographies, fun facts, and information about the first pets.

Worldmapper

http://www.sasi.group.shef.ac.uk/worldmapper/index.html

Containing more than 700 maps, some available as PDF posters, Worldmapper has a map for everyone. You can find population maps and maps according to worldwide Internet users, literacy, human poverty, and much more.

SOCIAL STUDIES
RESOURCES

FRUGAL FUN

Activities, Tips, and Games to Promote Social Studies Without Spending Money

Ancestor Tea Party

Make the past relevant by inviting students' ancestors to tea one day. Seek donations of tea cookies, tea bags, cups, plates, and napkins. Give students a week or two to talk with their families about an interesting ancestor, and have them come to tea dressed up as their relative one day. Invite students to introduce themselves to the class by telling whom they dressed as and why. Then, enjoy refreshments.

Children Like Me

Help children see that all children around the world have similarities and differences. Check out the book *Children Like Me* from the library, and share some things about the different children with your students. Point out similarities and differences. Have students work in small groups to create Venn diagrams comparing and contrasting themselves to a child in the book.

Community Play

An awareness of their greater community and how it all fits together is important for elementary students. Ask around to see if anyone has old puppets, dolls, LEGO characters, Little People figures, or other toys decorated as community workers. Designate a small play area for role-playing what these people do to build community.

Community Workers

Ask local workers—city officials, bus drivers, post office workers, etc.—to come in and talk to your students throughout the year about their jobs. You can also ask parents to take turns coming in to speak about what they do.

Compass Rose

Help your students learn their directions by making a compass rose to display in the classroom. Use electrical tape for this activity; it comes in various colors, is stretchy enough to be bent into circles, and pulls up cleanly. You can explain the activity in a letter home and ask for donated tape. With your students' help, move the desks and tables out of the center of the room, and tape a large circle. Then, add triangles to form the points of the compass rose. Finally, use the tape to label the directions and decorate it. You can connect this to reading an actual compass by having several students use compasses to check that your directions are correct.

Cookie Party

Read some of the book *Mistakes That Worked* by Charlotte Foltz Jones, and call your students' attention to the invention of the Toll House cookie. Have them work with a small group to "invent" their own cookie. Then, if desired, send a note home asking students to work with their parents to create a unique cookie to bring into school for a Cookie Invention Party. If you have allergies in your classroom, you could have each student make and present a model of his or her invented cookie out of clay or playdough instead.

Ethnic Foods Mapping

Prior to this activity, visit ethnic restaurants (or their websites) in your area and pick up or print their take-out menus. Remind your students that the United States is a melting pot of cultures and ask them to track down where ethnic restaurants from the area get their inspiration. Group the students in cooperative groups and give each group a few menus. Have them locate the origin of the cuisine on a map.

Invention Questions

When studying about inventors, bring in several different products from your home (i.e., lip balm, Swiffer dusters). Explain that all products were created to fill a need. Have your students work in small groups to try to come up with a reason an item was invented. Then, find the address of the company (usually on the packaging or website), and have each group write a letter asking about the product's origin.

Old Parchment Letters

Motivate your students to write about our founding fathers, explorers, or other people from the past by letting them write on "old parchment." Burn the edges of sheets of unlined paper, then soak them in tea. Allow them to dry before bringing them to class. Remind students to be very careful with their old paper!

Salt Dough Maps

This is one of those old-standby frugal ideas that has withstood the test of time because it works, it's fun, and kids love it. Mix up a batch of salt dough, first asking for supplies: Dissolve 1 cup salt in 1 1/4 cup warm water and add about 3 cups of flour. You'll need to make several batches depending on your planned usage and how many students you are using it with. Your students can make topography maps, landforms, volcanoes, and other features. Once the projects are built, let them sit out for a few days to harden. Then, allow students to paint their creations.

State ABCs

For those of you who teach about state history, try this fun project that uses materials you already have in your classroom and topics you're already teaching about. Either during or after the state study, have your students work cooperatively to create a page or pages for a state ABC book. Each letter will have its own page and facts related to both the state and letter will appear on that page. If your school has a binding machine available, use it to bind this into a class book when you are finished.

True Stories

Connect history to the personal with short picture book biographies about heroes of the past. Then ask your students to find out a true story about someone in their families' past to recount to the class. Take turns over the course of a few weeks to have students share their stories.

Vote!

Hold a mock election in your classroom during presidential or community races. Instead of buying the kits that are available from most teacher supply stores, make your own. Decorate a shoebox with red, white, and blue paper, and cut a slit in the top. Create ballots on the computer and print them. Make "I voted today!" stickers on mailing labels with clipart printed from your computer.

CHAPTER 7

HeaLTH anD PHYSICaL EDucaTIOn Resources

When I first began teaching in 1997, I taught third grade. My students had science, social studies, and health twice each week. I taught them health and wellness topics such as disaster preparedness and extreme weather safety (which I tied in to our science weather lessons to make each topic meatier), nutrition, and the human body, where we covered the body systems, how they function, and how they work together. Now, slightly more than a decade later, colleagues with whom I taught are no longer teaching health at that school. Several other local districts have dropped health topics from the curriculum and fit them in when they have time or schedule an assembly or field trip to cover nutrition or personal hygiene. Disaster preparedness is still taught briefly within the context of a larger weather unit—if science is still being taught.

Physical education programs are being cut as well. In some cases, P.E. teachers are responsible for teaching several classes of kids at a time, and in others, classroom teachers must now fit in some physical activity during the week. Additionally, recesses are being reduced or eliminated as districts are unable to hire aides, and teachers have more curricular demands put on them. There just isn't enough time in the day to cover everything.

If you are in a district that has seen these reductions firsthand, you know how difficult it is for kids to focus when they aren't able to get outside and run off some of their energy from time to time. You've thought again and again about how you can sneak a little physical education in, but you've come up short.

In this chapter, you'll find some resources that offer free curriculum ideas, games, lessons, and activities to get your kids moving. You'll find great ideas to help you bring health back into your days (or supplement that subject if you're still teaching it), and you'll be able to order posters and buttons to use as incentives for your students to keep them active and healthy. You will also find some easy-to-play games and tips for using transition times to get your kids up out of their seats. Be creative and have fun—and keep those kids moving!

The Always Changing Program

http://www.pgschoolprograms.com/puberty/index.php

Proctor and Gamble provides a complete curriculum to help you teach fifth-grade girls and boys about their changing bodies. The education kit must be approved by your school administrators before you order, and it will come with a DVD, printed teacher's guide, samples of Always pads and pantiliners, deodorant to use for demonstration, and a parent information postcard. In addition, girls will receive personal samples, a calendar for tracking their period, and a puberty education booklet. Boys will receive a puberty education booklet.

American Kennel Club

http://www.akc.org/kids_juniors/index.
cfm?nav_area=kids_juniors
http://www.akc.org/public_education/resources.cfm?page=4

The American Kennel Club believes that because dog ownership is such an integral part of our society, schoolchildren need to be educated about proper safety around dogs and how to care for their own dogs. The first link here goes to the page on their site dedicated to kids. There you'll find games and literature designed to help your kids learn more about pet ownership. The second link brings you specifically to the free resources page. Here you'll find two different education packs for which you can send away. One is about proper dog ownership and features a DVD of children teaching children how to take care of their new canine family members. It also includes a set of reproducibles and lesson plans. The second kit also includes a DVD, lesson plans, and reproducibles. This one, entitled *The Dog Listener*, teaches kids how to be safe around other people's dogs.

BrainPOP
http://www.brainpop.com/health

BrainPOP was created in 1999 by an immunologist to deliver tough information to his young patients in a creative, engaging, nonthreatening way. It now contains hundreds of short, standards-based animations on a variety of curriculum topics and can be used to introduce or supplement various units. Note that it is a subscription-based site, but it offers several videos in each subject area for free. This link will take you to the health video page.

Cabot Cheese
http://www.cabotcheese.coop/pages/
community_and_you/free_posters.php

Several really cool posters are available for free at the Cabot Cheese website. This is a fun way to encourage healthy choices like eating a good breakfast or making healthy snack choices. Posters could be hung in classrooms, cafeterias, or school hallways.

Campaign Publications and Materials
http://www.nichd.nih.gov/publications/pubskey.cfm?from=milk

Order free materials for teaching kids about the importance of milk in our diet from the National Institute of Child Health and Human Development. The program is Milk Matters, is available in English or Spanish, and includes coloring books, brochures, and posters.

CanolaInfo.org

https://canola-council.merchantsecure.com/canolainfo/store.aspx

CanolaInfo.org provides posters, booklets, and other materials to help kids learn about canola oil.

Centers for Disease Control and Prevention (CDC)

http://www.cdc.gov/education/teachers.html

The CDC lists links to help teachers and coaches find free resources for teaching kids to say no to tobacco and for keeping themselves healthy. There are also links to other types of curriculum, posters, activity sheets, DVDs, and more.

Clorox Classroom

http://www.clorox.com/classrooms/teachers/
resources-and-tips?exp=4#accordion

Help your students become members of the "Clean Team!" Clorox provides incentives, lesson plans, interactive whiteboard lessons, and more to help you teach your students how to fight germs and stay healthy.

Colgate Teachers

http://www.colgate.com/app/BrightSmilesBrightFutures/
US/EN/HomePage.cvsp

You'll find a collection of teacher's guides, activities, songs, take-home kits, mini posters, storybooks, notes for parents, and additional resources at the Colgate website.

HEALTH & P.E.
RESOURCES

Dole SuperKids
http://www.dole.com/SuperKids/Educators/
tabid/744/Default.aspx

Dole has long been committed to helping educate children to make healthy food choices. In the past, they've offered ABC fruit and vegetable cookbooks, coloring books, scripts for 40-minute musicals, soundtracks, and more. As of this writing, they're offering a Fruit and Vegetable Nutrition Facts Chart for upper elementary students. Additionally, they provide lesson plans for teachers and interactive games for students. This is a site worth bookmarking and checking back with a few times a year to see what's new. If you need to teach nutrition, you need this site.

The Dyslexic Reader
http://www.dyslexia.com/dysread.htm

The Dyslexic Reader is published quarterly by the Davis Dyslexia Association International. You can sign up to receive a free preview issue of this publication.

Earthquake Preparedness Handbook
https://sslearthquake.usgs.gov/regional/nca/handbook

Many teachers need to teach emergency preparedness as part of their health lessons, although some include it when they teach about weather or the Earth in science. Whichever route your lessons go, consider ordering copies of this handbook from the United States Geological Survey to distribute to students.

Egg Safety

http://www.aeb.org/foodservice-professionals/
egg-safety/egg-safety-material-order-form

The American Egg Board provides educational resources at no charge to teachers in the United States. Fill out the online order form, and you'll be sent a DVD, poster, and booklet.

Fairview Physical Education

http://fairviewpe.blogspot.com

This site is a blog maintained by a P.E. teacher in Michigan. He shares insight into his P.E. program, photographs, and tips. You'll find great ideas to help you make your P.E. lessons more engaging for your students.

Fuel Up to Play 60

http://www.fueluptoplay60.com

This program is designed to help students and teachers start a movement at school to eat healthier, get more active, and make a difference. This site has lots of great resources to help you decide if the program is right for you. Take some time to look through the site, then download the materials to get started.

Fun-Attic Game and Activity Guide

http://www.funattic.com/games.htm

There are some great game ideas on this site that use very inexpensive or free materials like rags and tennis balls. Search through the game-

of-the-month archives and develop a list of go-to games to play when your students need to get some energy out.

Goodcharacter.com Teaching Guides
http://www.goodcharacter.com/EStopics.html

Do you need to teach your students about developing good character? This site provides lots of resources to help you develop lessons and units. Here you'll find discussion questions, writing assignments, and activities for students in grades K–8.

Help Your Students Stay Healthy With Nose Care Tips From Puffs
http://www.pgschoolprograms.com/nose-care/index.php

Proctor and Gamble provides a complete curriculum to help you teach how the common cold is spread and how students can stay healthy by taking care of their noses. Depending on your state and local standards and curriculum guides, you may be able to adapt this resource up or down a grade level.

Kidd Safety
http://www.cpsc.gov/kids/kidsafety/index.html

This fun site is presented by the Consumer Product Safety Commission. The character, Kidd Safety, helps teach kids to use consumer products like bikes and toys safely through interactive games.

KidsHealth in the Classroom
http://kidshealth.org/classroom

KidsHealth in the Classroom provides free and complete curriculums for teaching health in the classroom. The teacher's guides can be downloaded along with handouts and games to use with the lessons.

Kids With Asthma Can!
http://www.pbs.org/parents/arthur/asthma/index.html

Using the characters from Marc Brown's popular Arthur series, PBS has created this valuable resource site for teaching kids about asthma. It includes audio and video clips, printables, and lesson plans.

Leafy Greens Council
http://www.leafy-greens.org

You can download resources, trading cards, coloring sheets, and lesson plans about nutritional and market information for produce at this site.

Milk Delivers Online Ordering
http://www.milkdelivers.org/online-ordering/#school-materials

This is the order page for Milk Delivers, an organization that encourages kids to drink more milk. You can order materials to hold flavored milk taste tests, incentives like sticker "milk mustaches," smiley buttons, and more. Everything here is free and ships to a valid school address. The site also offers posters and banners for a shipping fee.

HEALTH & P.E. RESOURCES

Mine Safety and Health Administration
http://www.msha.gov/KIDS/KIDSHP.HTM

The United States Department of Labor shares this page to help keep kids safe. Mines can seem so appealing to kids—dark, deep, mysterious, and dangerous. Of course, kids rarely realize the extent of danger involved in a mine. This page helps teach kids about the importance of staying out and safe. Definitely check it out if you have mines in your area.

Oral Deaf Education Resource Materials
http://www.oraldeafed.org/materials/index.html

For any teacher of a deaf student, this site is a welcome help. You can download booklets, CD-ROMs, and other materials to help you better teach your new student or help other students communicate effectively with their new friend.

Organic Valley: Order Your Kids' Activity Flyer
http://www.organicvalley.coop/resources/
educational-materials/kids-activity-flyer

By clicking on the "schools" link and filling out your information, you'll receive a bundle of 50 Kids Club activity books about eating organic foods. You'll also be able to sign up for Organic Valley's Farm Friends, which will earn you a welcome kit including coupons and additional informational resources.

PBS Teachers Health and Fitness

http://www.pbs.org/teachers/classroom/k-2/
health-fitness/resources
http://www.pbs.org/teachers/classroom/3-5/
health-fitness/resources

PBS Teachers provides detailed, standards-based resources for teaching health and fitness to elementary kids. The resources include interactive games, lesson plans, projects, videos, and more. All are clearly labeled by type and subject.

PE Central

http://www.pecentral.org

This is an award-winning site for health and physical education teachers. You'll find challenges to try with your students, lesson plans categorized by grade, games suggestions, teaching tips, and an online store.

PE Unit Plans

http://www.pelinks4u.org/links/unitplans.shtml

The online unit plans featured here were all created by P.E. majors at Central Washington University. Some are better than others, so make sure you preview them carefully before you decide to use one with your students.

Pete's PowerPoint Station

http://sports.pppst.com/index.html

http://science.pppst.com/humanbody/index.html

http://health.pppst.com/index.html

http://facs.pppst.com/safety.html

http://health.pppst.com/specialneedskids.html

Bursting with colorful graphics and tons of additional links, this is a website to return to again and again. PowerPoint presentations on just about every subject or topic taught to elementary students can be found at this site, along with bonus sections including free clipart and templates so you can create your own PowerPoints. If you have a projector or interactive whiteboard, this is a great site to go to when introducing a new topic of study.

Produce Oasis

http://www.produceoasis.com/Alpha_Folder/Alpha.html

Very cool site! Here you'll find an alphabetized list of fruits and vegetables and nutritional information for each fruit or vegetable.

Ready Kids

http://www.ready.gov/kids

If you need to teach disaster safety in your health class, this is a great resource for you. The Federal Emergency Management Agency has put together a collection of games, lessons, and activity sheets for you to help prepare your students for any disaster that may befall them.

Substance Abuse and Mental Health Services Administration: Publications Ordering
http://store.samhsa.gov/home

For teachers who work with kids suffering from mental health problems, support is important—for both them and the parents of the students themselves. The SAMHSA provides access to many free resources for teachers.

TeachFree.org
http://www.teachfree.org/
downelementaryschoolteachers_grades1-4_.aspx

This website is provided to educators by American Beef Producers through Cattleman's Beef Board and State Beef Councils. They research educational needs and produce teaching kits targeting those needs at various levels. This site includes reproducibles, downloadable songs, activity sheets, posters, and more.

Teaching Ideas: PE Warm-Up/Cool-Down Ideas
http://www.teachingideas.co.uk/pe/contents.htm

Here is a great list of warm-up and cool-down ideas for P.E. classes. These games could also be adapted for use in the classroom during transition times, after kids have sat for a long time, or when they just need to get their wiggles out.

Teachnet.com
http://teachnet.com/category/lessonplans/health

The mission of Teachnet.com is simple: to connect teachers and give them a voice. At this link, you'll find Teachnet.com's health and physical education activities. These are quick lessons, games, or tasks that can jump start your lessons, beef them up, add a hands-on component to a topic you're presenting, or just give the kids a break from worksheets.

Teach Your Students Nutrition Basics
http://www.pgschoolprograms.com/student-nutrition

Proctor and Gamble provides a complete curriculum to help you teach nutrition to fourth-grade students. Depending on your state and local standards and curriculum guides, you may be able to adapt this resource up or down a grade level.

USDA Food Safety Coloring Book
http://www.fsis.usda.gov/PDF/Mobile_Coloring_Book.pdf

Kids will learn how to fight back against "Bac" and other foodborne bacteria. This download can be used as individual activity sheets during a health unit or can be compiled into a coloring book.

Weekly Online Lessons
http://www.learnersonline.com/weekly/subject/health_pe.htm

The weekly online lesson archive is just one example of Learners Online's commitment to helping teachers and families find online materials. Each week, it presents math topics based on current events and highlights links to further resources.

WeissIce.com
http://weissice.com

This site is a fabulous resource to help educators shake up their lessons a bit. The author's approach to teaching P.E. is starting with fun, original games, then building on the fun with social education and movement.

What Is Braille?
http://www.afb.org/braillebug/Braille.asp

The American Foundation for the Blind has several interesting resources explaining what Braille is, how it was invented, how it is like any other code, and the logic needed for using it. You can go to this site and order a single Braille card for your own use or request a bulk order for distribution in your classroom. Use this resource to teach about differences and tolerance in health or social studies or about code breaking and logic in mathematics.

Yoga-Recess in Schools
http://www.yoga-recess.org

Yoga-Recess in Schools has put together a DVD for PreK/K students and those ages 7–16. They are currently working on a DVD for elementary school kids and teachers to use during recess. Use the online order form to select the DVD that would be best for your students.

Frugal Fun

Activities, Tips, and Games to Promote Health and Physical Education Without Spending Money

Dance Your Way Into the Day

Are you confident enough to be really silly with your students from time to time? If your morning is not getting off to a great start, you're tired and overwhelmed, your students are "off," and you have a full day of learning that you need to get sunk into little heads . . . jump start (or dance start) your day. Turn on the music, preferably music with a strong beat, and wiggle, jump, and dance. A few kids will look at you in a strange way (maybe more than a few), but then grab the hand of the nearest kiddo, and make him jump around, too. Then grab another, inviting all of them to shake off the morning slump. Wiggle, giggle, and groove, then slowly reduce the volume of the music, slow your movements, and ask the kids to pull out whatever they need for the first lesson. Now that you've gotten their "juices flowing," they'll be ready to focus.

Dental Health

Many pediatric dentists will come into classes to talk to kids about the proper way to take care of their teeth and gums—and often they'll hand out free toothbrushes and toothpaste. Be careful when you ask someone to come in, though. I've had several dentists speak to my kids. Most of them were wonderful. They truly wanted to teach kids about teeth. A few were only there to drum up business, though. All of the freebies they passed out had their name and phone number boldly printed, they dispersed literature about what might happen if your kids don't go to the dentist regularly, and they offered "free cleaning" coupons hidden in goody bags. Although I know that it is a reality in our world, I am uncomfortable with advertising directly to and through kids. When I invite someone into my classroom, I want him or her to improve a child's life or learning; I don't want the person to peddle to a student. My classroom newsletter always explained who our speakers were and where they worked. If parents want to contact them from that point, that's great. I like supporting people who give back. Just be leery when you invite someone in that the person isn't using it for a cheap advertising gimmick.

Do the Limbo!

Incorporate some fun physical activity during transitions or when your students seem particularly lethargic. Turn on some music, set a broomstick between bookcases, and have your students form a line and limbo to switch activities. Alternatively, you could place a string across your doorway with tape and have your students "limbo off to lunch!"

Fresh Air

Sometimes, all you need is fresh air to get yourself going again. Whenever you can, take your students outside. You can conduct lessons out there, read books, have silent reading time, or go for a walk. The main thing is to get the kids outside regularly. If you have time, you can add some easy games like Red Light, Green Light; Red Rover; Tag; and others.

Germ Detective

When teaching young children about the importance of washing their hands, your words often fall on deaf ears. Show them the importance next time. You could do this in several ways. If the health department in your area is willing to come and talk to your students for free, ask if they could make a presentation about how germs are spread and how hand washing can help. Ask them if they have a fluorescent light they can bring with them. Invite students to wash their hands, and then have the health official run the light near their "clean" hands. Students (especially those who just rinsed under water) will be amazed at the germs that light up—still on their hands! Alternatively, if you are able to find an inexpensive handheld fluorescent light, it might be worth purchasing because they last for so long. I found a small light (about

1 1/2" x 3") at a store called Five Below. It's like a dollar store that offers items for $5 or less. It routinely carries science kits for kids. My fluorescent light was in a forensic science kit, cost $5, and contained materials for fingerprint dusting and more. Keep your eyes open for deals like these. You can spend a few dollars and repurpose things for several subjects.

Musical Chairs

This no-cost game is a favorite of kids of all ages (even if they won't admit it). It's got it all—movement, music, and cutthroat competition. Set up some chairs—one fewer than the number of players—turn on some music, and let them circle the chairs. When the music stops, everyone needs to sit down. The player standing is out. Start the music again, kids start their circling, and you remove another chair (or chairs if you want the game to go faster). Play continues until only one student is left standing. Have the remaining students stand on the sidelines and cheer on their classmates.

CHAPTER 8

Art and Music Resources

Looking back over the years and the cycle of wealth and recession in our public schools, we see that art and music programs are often some of the first to be cut when times get tough. The fine arts are very important, though, and teachers know it. Whether you are a classroom teacher or a special area teacher, you know that when kids are given the chance to be creative with art and music, they thrive.

Creativity makes for happy kids, and happy kids are better able to learn. In addition to kids' creativity being fostered and developed by the arts, their brains are cultivated as well. When a child is able to use his mind to think abstractly and is given a chance to express himself freely, he becomes a more creative thinker in general. This leads to greater problem-solving skills and an inquisitive spirit—two traits that are essential in science, technology, engineering, and math.

The arts and sciences go hand in hand. A creative and critical mind solves problems by seeing things others do not. It can see beneath the surface and get to the root of an issue. It is the mind of one who may become a future leader. We need to make sure that we find ways to allow kids to get their music and art, even when those programs are cut. And we need to find ways to do it without continuing to overburden classroom teachers in terms of time and money.

Think about what makes a rich learning experience for your students, and begin your search there. If you're teaching a science unit about volcanoes, you may want to display some artwork depicting past eruptions, or find an art project for your students to do that is different from the typical baking-soda volcano you've always done. How about having kids follow the directions for making their own papyrus you found on an art project idea blog when you're teaching ancient history? Or you might be able to find some Mexican music to download for your Cinco de Mayo celebration.

This chapter provides some resources for finding inspiration online and resources from outside sources. Comb your community, too. Approach local businesses and ask if you can have their used copy paper for kids to draw on. Look through library and garage sales for drawing books, and set up an art center that students can visit throughout the day. Integrate art into each subject you teach. Plot points on graph paper to form a picture, or make a pharaoh's mask out of clay when you teach about Egypt. When you are learning math facts, play some CDs that sing the facts. You can find songs online in a variety of genres—country/western, rock, and more. When you are teaching world geography, find traditional songs to play from each country. Use this chapter as a jumping-off point and build from there.

Alex's Paper Airplanes
http://www.paperairplanes.co.uk

This is a cool site! Short videos and instructions show and tell visitors how to make really amazing paper airplanes with a few folds. Have an airplane-design lesson and talk about aesthetics and aerodynamics—it will be really fun!

Annenberg Learner: Arts
http://learner.org/resources/browse.html?discipline=1

From the Annenberg Foundation, this site provides an index of videos on how to teach just about any art subject. There are online video workshops for teachers, as well as videos from which students would benefit. It may take you a while to navigate the site at first, but you'll find some gems here.

Art Junction
http://artjunction.org

Art Junction is an outreach project of the Art Education Program of the University of Florida. You can find art activities and projects to help you teach drawing, painting, and art appreciation.

Art Lessons for Kids
http://artlessonsforkids.wordpress.com

Ms. Ale is an art teacher working in elementary schools overseas. She shares art ideas and lessons and also offers nominally priced eBooks on her site.

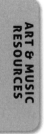

Art With Mr. E
http://artwithmre.blogspot.com

This is a fun art class blog. Mr. E is creative, colorful, and a bit wacky, and he offers wonderful resources for the classroom—management ideas, lesson plans, and kids' projects.

Artcyclopedia
http://www.artcyclopedia.com

This is an incredible database of artwork listed by the artist's name. With this site, you can easily integrate the lives of famous painters, glassmakers, engravers, inventors, sculptors, potters, and more into your everyday lessons.

Artists Helping Children Arts and Crafts
http://www.artistshelpingchildren.org

This is a huge resource for kids and teachers. You'll find drawing lessons, coloring sheets, arts and crafts project ideas, and much, much more.

Artsology
http://artsology.com

This comprehensive site includes investigations like, "How do artists depict motion?," as well as games and other activities related to art and music. It also shares incredible artwork by children of all ages.

ArtsWork

http://artswork.asu.edu/arts/teachers/index.htm

This is a collection of art lesson plans, resources links, and organization information for art teachers at all levels.

Artyfactory

http://artyfactory.com

Free art lessons that use many different media can be found at this great site. You can teach your students to create pencil drawings, work on perspective, and more.

BBC Schools Music

http://www.bbc.co.uk/schools/websites/4_11/site/music.shtml

The BBC provides a collection of lessons and games for various subjects. At this link, you'll find loads of interactive games that teach music. Remember that this is a British website, though, and preview each game before allowing your students to play it. Some British word usages may be different than American usages.

BrainPOP

http://www.brainpop.com/artsandmusic

BrainPOP was created in 1999 by an immunologist to deliver tough information to his young patients in a creative, engaging, nonthreatening way. It now contains hundreds of short, standards-based animations on a variety of curriculum topics and can be used to introduce or supplement various units. Note that it is a subscription-based site, but it offers several videos in each subject area for free. This link will take you to the arts and music video page.

Bright Ring Art Activities
http://brightring.com/Fun%20Activities.html

For more than 25 years, Bright Ring Publications has been creating activity books that focus on art as a process, not a product. At this link, you'll find several free activities to try out with your students.

Chunky Monkey's Cartoon Lessons
http://www.chunkymonkey.com/howto/drawinglessons.htm

Lessons at this site, both in video and written form, teach young kids how to draw cartoon-like animals.

Cool Curriculum
http://www.uic.edu/classes/ad/ad382/
sites/Projects/P_index.html

The Cool Curriculum link at Spiral Art Education includes art ideas and lessons for art students in kindergarten through college.

Craftbits
http://www.craftbits.com

You won't want to turn your students loose on this site, as some of the projects aren't really appropriate for school, but you can find some fun and easy ways to use old items to create neat, quirky gifts. Maybe you're looking for something to do with your students to celebrate

their parents during the holidays. Or you might want to find a unique way to commemorate a theme unit. Whatever your reason, there are some unique projects at this site.

Danielle's Place
http://daniellesplace.com

This site is loaded with suggestions for using crafts and teaching history, culture, and other academic topics. The author of this site is Christian and includes Bible verses with some of her crafts and activities, but this can easily be adapted if you teach in a traditional public school or a religious school of different beliefs. The craft ideas were too cute and too original to leave this resource out of this book.

Dick Blick Featured Disciplines
http://www.dickblick.com/lesson-plans/discipline

No doubt you've ordered supplies from Dick Blick's amazing catalog of art materials, but did you know that the company offers free lesson plans for download on its site? Organized by topics such as clay, paper, collage, and mask making, you're sure to find something to enhance any topic you're teaching.

Disney Family Fun
http://familyfun.go.com

This companion site to Disney's Family Fun Magazine contains thousands of activities, crafts, and easy-to-make games that you can adapt to your classroom.

Draw and Color With Uncle Fred
http://unclefred.com

On this site, the Uncle Fred character teaches quick, easy-to-master demonstrations of cartoon art. Young kids especially will feel like real artists after giving these lessons a try.

Drawspace
http://www.drawspace.com

On this site, run by a former police sketch artist, you'll find dozens of free and beautifully illustrated drawing lessons to engage students of all abilities.

Elmer's Crafters' Projects
http://www.elmers.com/crafters/projects

This page, offered by the makers of Elmer's Glue, shares many fun and eye-catching projects for you to do with your students.

Everything in Papercrafting Special Paper Promotion
http://everythinginpapercrafting.com/paper_promotion.html

The message on this sample-request page states what I'm sure many of us have felt when embarking on a new hobby: "Don't wanna spend money on the craft before you know you like it?" Their offer is generous (and smart): Fill out the request form, and they'll send you a 50-sheet pack of origami paper in three sizes, enough to make all of the free designs they share on their site. They don't even charge shipping! All they ask in return is that if you enjoy the craft, you think about ordering additional supplies from them in the future. I received this pack, and my kids and I have had fun folding paper animals ever since. The quality is wonderful, the colors are bright, and we will definitely purchase from them when our 50-pack runs out!

Favecrafts
http://www.favecrafts.com/#

Favecrafts is a blog that offers loads of free craft ideas and templates. On a rotating basis, it offers free downloadable eBooks and sewing, crochet, or knitting patterns. Bookmark this site and check back regularly to download its latest eBook offerings.

ART & MUSIC RESOURCES

Free Glue From Ringtonica
http://www.ringtonica.com/multi_glue

Ringtonica is a site that sells ringtones for cell phones. This free sample—to advertise their website and products—is completely free, so I thought it worth including. Who can't use a free bottle of glue in an elementary classroom?

Free Children's Music
http://freekidsmusic.com

The folks at Free Children's Music got some great artists together to provide full-length songs for free download. You'll find everything from "Shoelace Soup" by Jam Toast to "The Alphabet Song."

Glue Dots Free Sample

http://www.buygluedots.com/free_glue_dot_samples.html
Gate Way Distributors, Inc
13591 McGregor Blvd #19
Fort Myers, FL 33919

Its website suggests that users "send us a self-addressed, stamped envelope, and a description of your application for the glue dots, and samples will be provided." If you've never used Glue Dots before, check them out. They're fabulous for most craft projects, and I use them regularly when I scrapbook.

The Imagination Factory

http://kid-at-art.com

Join the Imagination Factory from Columbus, IN, online as you allow your students to set their imaginations loose. There are art lessons in drawing, sculpture, painting, holidays, printmaking, fiber arts, collage, marbling, and crafts. You can even allow your students to decorate their own Flat Stanley and start an exchange program!

Incredible Art Department

http://princetonol.com/groups/iad

Start with the lessons link here, navigate through to find great lesson-planning ideas, and then check out the art history and free time activity links. There you'll find even more teaching ideas. This site is maintained by Princeton University.

Instructables
http://www.instructables.com/index

This is crafting and science all rolled together! You can find directions here for helping your students make a simple reading lamp (studying electrical circuits?), a box kite (aerodynamics?), and much more.

The J. Paul Getty Museum: Education
http://getty.edu/education

The museum provides a scope and sequence, lesson plans, curriculum ideas, online galleries, discussion areas, a reading room, and more to help you develop a successful art curriculum for your school or classroom.

Kids and Teens: Arts—Photography
http://www.dmoz.org/Kids_and_Teens/Arts/Photography

Do you have any budding photographers in your midst? Help foster that creative spirit with this compendium of online photography lesson plans that cover topics from the basics of cameras all the way through composition and getting a unique shot.

KinderArt
http://kinderart.com

This website is a wonderful resource for K–12 teachers of every subject. There are lots of lesson plans covering every form of art including architecture, crafts, painting, printmaking, and more. It's easy to navigate and user friendly. You can find an art project to accompany just about any topic you need to teach.

Local Learning
http://locallearningnetwork.org

Local Learning began as a local folk art group and has grown to encompass more communities. At the site, you can learn more about folk art, as well as use the biographies of folk artists to inspire kids to create their own work.

Matisse & Picasso
http://www.matisse-picasso.org

This website offers a teacher resource pack including reproductions of five paintings and lesson plans, along with a resource guide for teachers. It guides you through the gentle competition that these two amazing artists had with one another.

Music at School
http://www.musicatschool.co.uk/index.htm

This great website teaches music using online lessons, tutorials, printable worksheets, and quizzes. There are also links available for further study.

Music Education Online
http://www.childrensmusicworkshop.com

Children's Music Workshop presents online articles, videos, information about specific instruments (including how to choose one of your own), and links to additional resources on the web.

My Craft Book
http://mycraftbook.com

This is a nice collection of crafts organized by occasion and age group.

National Gallery of Art Learning Resources
http://www.nga.gov/education/learningresources/index.shtm

The National Gallery of Art offers free loaner materials to teachers across the country. At this page, you can search by curriculum area, subject, or artist to find paintings, CDs, DVDs, and more, all available to borrow. The NGA asks that you request your materials at least one month in advance to give them enough time to locate, prepare, and ship the materials. Other than that, you keep them as long as you need, and pay minimal return shipping.

Online Etch A Sketch
http://ohioart.com

Okay, this one's just for fun. Remember the challenge of creating legible art on your old Etch A Sketch? Now, Ohio Art brings you a free online version. Click on the link at the bottom-left side of the page and get creating!

The Papier Mache Resource
http://www.papiermache.co.uk

Learn how to successfully make papier-mache sculptures, and browse the gallery for inspiration.

Pete's PowerPoint Station

http://art.pppst.com/index.html
http://architecture.pppst.com/index.html
http://music.pppst.com/index.html
http://theatre.pppst.com/index.html

Bursting with colorful graphics and tons of additional links, this is a website to return to again and again. PowerPoint presentations on just about every subject or topic taught to elementary students can be found at this site, along with bonus sections including free clipart and templates so you can create your own PowerPoints. If you have a projector or interactive whiteboard, this is a great site to go to when introducing a new topic of study.

Print-n-Play Toys

http://www.mcguirezone.com/goodies/toys.html

These fun paper games are easy to print and build. Your students will have fun creating the working games out of paper and cardstock.

Refrigerator to Renoir: Great Art Lessons on the Net

http://www.educationworld.com/a_lesson/lesson106.shtml

Education World shares this article about teaching art to kids and includes links to 10 fun and interactive art lessons online.

Ricci Adams' Musictheory.net
http://www.musictheory.net

This is a great website for teaching the basics of music. You'll find animated lessons that explore music fundamentals, exercises so students can practice what they've learned, and tools to help them calculate notes.

San Diego Museum of Art: Education
http://www.sdmart.org/education

The San Diego Museum of Art presents a collection of art lesson plans for projects that can be developed from inexpensive materials and are easy to integrate into a variety of disciplines.

The San Francisco Symphony Kids
http://www.sfskids.org/templates/home.asp?pageid=1

This is one of the coolest free music resources I came across. SFS Kids teaches about the instruments of the orchestra and where they are located on stage, and there's a music lab that teaches kids about everything music, from the basics to creating their own compositions. Finally, there is a radio feature that allows kids to listen to the symphony play.

Simpler Pleasures Fabric
http://www.simplerpleasures.com/sample606.ccml

Use this online sample request form to order a pack of fabric swatches. Fabric comes in handy for lot of different projects: collages, book binding, small sewing projects, and more.

Sound Junction

http://www.soundjunction.org/default.aspa

Here, you'll find many different genres of music to explore, and your students can learn about rhythm, harmony, melody, and texture. There also are biographies and links to learn about musicians, their careers, and much more.

Teachnet.com

http://teachnet.com/category/lessonplans/art
http://teachnet.com/category/lessonplans/music

The mission of Teachnet.com is simple: to connect teachers and give them a voice. At this link, you'll find Teachnet.com's art activities. These are quick lessons, games, or tasks that can jumpstart your lessons, beef them up, add a hands-on component to a topic you're presenting, or just give the kids a break from worksheets.

Toad Hollow Studio Drawing Lessons

http://www.toadhollowstudio.com

Teaching online drawing lessons since 1999, Toad Hollow Studio offers more than 20 lessons that teach students gradation, smoothing, and other techniques.

The Toymaker

http://thetoymaker.com

This is one of my family's favorite sites on the Internet! Here, you can print and build (out of plain paper) toys that move, math toys, gift boxes, animal toys, and more. Fold them up, tape them securely, and you have a new toy to play with!

Weekly Online Lessons
http://www.learnersonline.com/weekly/subject/art.htm

The weekly online lesson archive is just one example of Learners Online's commitment to helping teachers and families find online materials. Each week, it presents topics based on current events and highlights links to further resources.

Winsor & Newton Acrylics Free Samples
http://acrylics.winsornewton.com/en/samples/requestsamples

Winsor & Newton, maker of artist-quality acrylic paints, occasionally offers free paint samples to artists. Check back and fill out the request form as often as you can.

World Wide Arts Resources
http://wwar.com

This is an incredibly comprehensive site featuring contemporary art news, history, artist information, and portfolios, along with interactive links and videos.

Yamaha Paper Crafts
http://www.yamaha-motor.co.jp/global/entertainment/papercraft

Download, cut, fold, and tape/glue these realistic models together with your students. This activity is sure to be a lot of fun and is very boy friendly.

Frugal Fun

**Activities, Tips, and Games
to Promote Art and Music
Without Spending Money**

Antiqued Vase

If you're looking for a unique present for students to make for Mother's Day, try this. Ask for bottle donations. Glass, Perrier, soda, or even interestingly shaped condiment bottles are perfect. Also ask if anyone has a partially used container of brown shoe polish you could have. You'll want to have several on hand. Have students cover their bottles in a criss-cross fashion with pieces of masking tape cut into varying lengths. Then, ask them to lightly rub the shoe polish over the tape once the bottle is completely covered.

Composer of the Month

Play music in the background during the day. Enhance students' music appreciation by choosing a famous classical composer and reading a short biography about the person before introducing the music. (Music and biographies of classical composers can usually be downloaded for free on the Internet.)

Gathering Used Supplies

At the end of each school year, I noticed students throwing their used crayons, markers, glue, and even scissors away. I was disturbed at the wastefulness of this because when I brought it up with students, they informed me that because they get new supplies at the beginning of each school year anyway, there was no point in keeping these. So I sent a note home explaining the observation and conversation to parents and asked them to reply: If it was all right (or even expected) for their kids to throw their supplies away, would they give permission for me to keep them for future use instead? Almost all of the parents agreed, and I sent that letter home every year. On desk clean-out day, I'd put out labeled plastic containers and tell students that if they planned to throw away their supplies, they should sort them into the containers instead.

Hand-Me-Down Instruments

If your music department is upgrading its instruments, ask if you can have some of the tambourines and cymbals. Have students play short rhythms to signal subject changes, or play musical patterns during math or class meetings.

Ideas for Using Donated Supplies

- Put tubs of used crayons, markers, colored pencils, glue, and scissors, along with paper and scraps, out on a table for students to use when they have free time. The creativity is usually quite impressive.
- Donate them to an inner-city school.
- Melt the crayons for fun art projects. We just did a great project that I read about on several different blogs and websites. I bought an inexpensive artist's canvas from the craft store with a 40% off coupon ($5 after coupon), hot glued crayons across the top in rainbow order, propped up the crayon-canvas on newspaper, and gave the kids each a hairdryer. They held the dryers to the crayons until they melted in colorful streams down the front of the canvas, mixing and melding together. It turned out really cool, used crayon scraps I had laying around, and provided a great focal point for our playroom. We're already planning another, personalized one for an art-loving friend's ninth birthday!

Photographing Patterns

Tie math and art together by using one of your school's digital cameras with your students. Send them around the building in twos and threes and ask them to photograph any interesting patterns they see. Have them download and print their pictures, mount them on cardstock or construction paper, and share them with the class. Finally, create a bulletin board display of your students' work.

Recycled Instruments

Have your students make rubber band guitars, oatmeal can drums, and pie tin tambourines. There are directions for instruments made out of recycled materials all over the Internet. Find some, ask parents to send in materials (after all, it is trash!), and let students decide which they want to make. Form a recycled-instrument band, and play for other classes or for parents.

CHAPTER 9

Teachers' Blogs

Teachers are generous and creative people. On the Internet you can find blogs about so many things; chances are that if you have an interest or a hobby, there is someone blogging about it. Teaching is no different. In this chapter, I've included some of my favorite teacher blogs. Some offer advice, some tell stories from the trenches, some focus on the politics in our current educational climate, and others offer fabulous, fun, and free ideas about how you can make your classroom a better place for you and your students.

Enjoy these glimpses into other people's classrooms. Teaching is all about sharing ideas, so take the seeds you find and tweak them to fit your situation and your personality. There truly is something for everyone in this chapter.

2 Cents' Worth
http://davidwarlick.com/2cents

Educator David Warwick shares insights about how new technology can help you better serve your students.

Adventures of First Grade
http://adventuresoffirstgrade.blogspot.com

Fabulous ideas and links fill this blog. The author shares pictures from her own classroom, behavior management ideas, craft projects, and more.

Bit By Bit
http://bobsprankle.com/bitbybit_wordpress

Bob Sprankle is an elementary technology integrator. His blog features ideas for integrating technology into your classroom.

Bryant's Brain Train
http://bryantsbraintrain.blogspot.com

The Bryant family shares tips on teaching, parenting, and helping kids achieve. Shannon, a veteran teacher, also offers creative curriculum and ideas.

Cathy Jo Nelson's Professional Thoughts
http://blog.cathyjonelson.com

Cathy Jo Nelson is a library media specialist and hosts this blog to help teachers and librarians learn to integrate "technology in an authentic and ethical manner in the name of increasing student engagement." She posts on "techno Tuesdays" and offers opinions and responses to questions she's been asked or news articles or new technology she's come across.

Chets Math Homework Help
http://chetsmath.blogspot.com

A second- and third-grade math teacher shares this blog to demystify the way math is taught now so that parents can feel more confident when they help their children with their math homework. It's a great

TEACHERS' BLOGS

tool for helping teachers see other ways of presenting the same material. This blog hasn't been updated in a while, but it's still worth checking out for the richness of resources and teaching ideas.

Cool Cat Teacher Blog
http://coolcatteacher.blogspot.com

A love of technology has led this teacher to develop an award-winning blog, present at educational conferences all around the world, and write a book. She blogs about education and technology.

Daisy Yellow
http://daisyyellow.squarespace.com

This blog offers fun, accessible ways to get kids hooked on art.

Deep Space Sparkle
http://www.deepspacesparkle.com

You'll find tons of art lessons and reviews on supplies at this blog. The art teacher who hosts it includes lots of bright and engaging photos of student artwork.

Dynamite Lesson Plan
http://www.dynamitelessonplan.com

The author of this blog maintains that it is a dynamite lesson plan that truly makes teaching work. If you engage your students, you won't need to worry about discipline, because the kids will be too busy to misbehave. He offers lesson-planning tips and commentary on educational issues.

Eduflack
http://blog.eduflack.com

Learn better communication skills for dealing with parents and colleagues on this blog.

TEACHERS' BLOGS

Elementary Education
http://k6educators.about.com/b

This blog from About.com offers tips and ideas from a teacher that will help you as you plan and manage your lessons.

Elementary Education Blog (ElEdBlog)
http://eledblog.com

At this site, teachers can join a community of teacher bloggers by following along with the various conversations or starting a blog of their own.

Elementary Science
http://cicobb.typepad.com/es

This blog is meant to keep science teachers in Georgia updated on special programs and events, but it contains great information for any science teacher.

F Is for First Grade
http://fisforfirstgrade.blogspot.com

This first-grade teacher shares some of her favorite ideas, lessons, and activities from around the web and her own classroom.

Funny First-Grade People
http://www.funny-first-grade-people.com/index.html

This great blog provides helpful resources and hilarious conversations between the teacher, Lynda Smith Davis, and the little people in her classroom. Lots to navigate and chuckle your way through!

A Geeky Momma's Blog
http://www.leekolbert.com

Don't let the name fool you; this blog is education centered and well written. Lee Kolbert is the district manager of the Department of Educational Technology in Florida after teaching in the classroom and other positions for more than 25 years. She shares technology-integration insights and her thoughts on education in general.

Gifted Exchange
http://giftedexchange.blogspot.com

This is a blog about gifted education and advocacy for gifted kids. It presents current research and problems facing education as a whole.

Ginger Snaps
http://gingersnapstreatsforteachers.blogspot.com

This is a very cute blog hosted by a third-grade teacher. She has tons of fun and creative ideas to share, and you get a chance to look inside her classroom often.

Heidisongs Resource
http://heidisongs.blogspot.com

Kindergarten teacher Heidi Butkus created a curriculum for innovative kindergarten teaching and shares some of it, along with her day-to-day life in the classroom, on this blog.

History Is Elementary
http://historyiselementary.blogspot.com

Written by an elementary teacher, this blog can help you breathe new life into your social studies curriculum.

I Want to Teach Forever
http://www.teachforever.com

You'll find thoughts, insights, and clever ideas about math, social studies, and teaching in general on this blog.

Kindergarten's 3 R's: Respect, Resources, and Rants
http://kidney-garden.blogspot.com

Michaele Sommerville is a wonderful blogger. She offers stories from her classroom, quotes from her students, practical ideas, and lesson plans.

Learning Is Messy
http://learningismessy.com/blog

Brian Crosby is an innovative and opinionated teacher who tells it like it is and shares the fabulous things he and his students are doing. This blog is filled with examples of kids doing great things and talk of all things education.

The Lesson Machine
http://thelessonmachine.com/blog

This online magazine blog offers tips for everything education. It is technically written for teachers of all grade levels, but hosts tons of articles for elementary teachers.

Literacy and Laughter
http://literacyandlaughter.blogspot.com

This blog has tons of creative, fun ideas for making your classroom a fun place for your students to be.

Michael Smith's Principals Page
http://www.principalspage.com/theblog

Michael Smith started his career as a teacher and a coach, then moved into a position as K–12 principal. He is now a superintendent and blogs about education and administration.

Mrs. Cassidy's Classroom Blog
http://classblogmeister.com/blog.php?blogger_id=1337

Kathy Cassidy and her first-grade students in Canada invite visitors into their classroom via this blog. Students blog on their own pages, Mrs. Cassidy offers tutorials on things they've done in her class, and lots of videos and pictures are posted so you can see exactly how lessons played out.

Mrs. Jump's Class
http://mrsjumpsclass.blogspot.com

There are some great ideas on this blog, along with inspiration and lots of bright colors!

Mrs. Meacham's Classroom Snapshots
http://mrsmeachamclassroom.wordpress.com

Jessica Meacham hosts this blog and its companion website at http://www.jmeacham.com. She has taught every grade from K–6, and shares all of the amazing and creative things she does. This is a site that every teacher should bookmark!

No Limits 2 Learning
http://nolimitstolearning.blogspot.com

This educator works with innovative and assistive technology to help special needs students and their teachers and occupational therapists use them.

Peg's Plans
http://pegsplans.blogspot.com

The author of this blog shares her upper elementary lesson plans for language arts, math, and science. She also shares homework, art, project, and game ideas.

A Place Called Kindergarten
http://aplacecalledkindergarten.blogspot.com

The author of this blog invites others in to take a peek at what she and her students do every day. She also shares links to other great resources online.

The Public School Insights Blog
http://www.learningfirst.org/blog

Presented by the Learning First Alliance, this blog updates readers on the current state of public education and issues related to teaching and teachers.

Reading With Mrs. Bast
http://dbast.edublogs.org

Mrs. Bast is a reading teacher who works with first- and third-grade readers. Her blog is written to help teachers inspire kids to become lifelong learners.

Regurgitated Alpha Bits
http://regurgitatedalphabits.blogspot.com

This fun blog takes a look at the humor in teaching and shares great ideas and links to others' ideas on the Internet.

A Special Kind of Class
http://aspecialkindofclass.blogspot.com

This blog contains wonderful wisdom from a special education teacher about how to work with and treat kids with disabilities or other special needs in your class.

Starting Our Journey
http://www.startingourjourney.com

Mrs. Hawley shares links, thoughts, and suggestions for her kindergartners' parents. There's a lot to be gleaned from her blog.

Steve Spangler Science
http://www.stevespangler.com

Steve Spangler was an elementary science teacher and is now a media sensation. He performs fun, cool science experiments on local news channels, writes books, devises new challenges, offers teacher workshops, and has a really cool shop of all things science. This blog shows some of his greatest "pranks" and experiments in video format and gives you easy things to do with kids to get them excited about science.

Stories From School
http://www.storiesfromschool.org

Real teachers who are board certified and highly qualified weigh in on issues facing education today and offer great insights on this blog.

Surviving a Teacher's Salary
http://www.survivingateacherssalary.com

Written by the stay-at-home wife of a second-grade teacher, this blog offers deals, freebies, and reviews of products and things to make your life more fun, more educational, and less expensive. It's cute, engaging, and fun to navigate.

Taming the Octopus
http://tamingtheoctopus-themanyarmsofwriting.blogspot.com

Taming the Octopus is a fabulous resource for helping you guide your kids to becoming better writers.

Teach a Gifted Kid
http://teachagiftedkid.com

This is a great blog written by the mom of two gifted boys, wife of a gifted husband, and teacher to many gifted students. She will challenge your thinking on how gifted kids think and learn, and she will remind you that these kids have very unique needs.

Teacher Bits and Bobs
http://teacherbitsandbobs.blogspot.com

Two very creative teachers host this blog full of craft ideas and more about teaching in the elementary schools. You'll find inspiration and lots of great ideas here.

Teacher to Teacher
http://blogs.scholastic.com/classroom_solutions

Hosted by Scholastic, these blogs, Top Teaching and Classroom Solutions, are written by a team of teacher advisors. They offer solutions and suggestions for any issue or lesson an elementary teacher may face.

Teachers Love SMART Boards
http://smartboards.typepad.com/smartboard

This blog, created by James Hollis in 2007, covers all things SMART board. Here you'll find tutorials, lessons, games, and activities all designed to help you utilize the interactive whiteboard in your classroom.

Teaching Blog Addict
http://www.teachingblogaddict.com

This blog has many contributors, making it a rich one-stop shop for printables, theme units, and special projects to use in your home-school or classroom.

Teaching Challenges
http://teachingchallenges.blogspot.com

Australian teacher Penny Ryder shares her solutions to overcoming the challenges sometimes associated with teaching. Go to this blog for inspiration and encouragement.

The Teaching Palette
http://theteachingpalette.com

Hillary Andrlik and Theresa McGee, two art teachers from the Chicago area, founded this blog that focuses on "arteducationology," or the study of art education. They cover classroom management and music and art integration, and they feature product reviews.

That Little Art Teacher
http://ms-artteacher.blogspot.com

What a super-cute blog! It is hosted by a PreK–6 art teacher in Tennessee. She shares ideas, projects, and classroom management strategies that will work for any teacher.

TEACHERS'
BLOGS

Think Like a Teacher
http://blog.teachersfirst.com/thinkteach

You'll find tips for teachers, education news, and commentary about the state of education at this popular blog.

Thoughts By Jen
http://projectsbyjen.com/blog

There are some wonderful and exciting projects that integrate technology and teach a variety of skills to both teachers and their students on this blog. It is very easy to get caught up on reading about all of the fun projects you and your students could take part in.

Two Writing Teachers
http://twowritingteachers.wordpress.com

These writers really know their stuff! You'll find fabulous resources and tips for teaching writing to kids here. Ruth Ayres and Stacey Shubitz have written numerous books and presented at countless workshops, and they blog to empower and inspire other writing teachers.

What the Teacher Wants
http://whattheteacherwants.blogspot.com

This blog has something for all elementary teachers. It is written by two teachers—one first grade and the other fifth. So, it covers all sorts of ideas, plans, and projects that can be adapted across grade levels.

What Works in Education
http://www.edutopia.org

This is the blog of the George Lucas Educational Foundation. It covers everything current in education, hosts a variety of subject-specific blogs and conversations, and helps connect teachers to strategies and resources that work.

Will Richardson
http://willrichardson.com

Will Richardson, an educator, speaker, and author, writes this blog about education and learning. A great read.

A Year of Reading
http://readingyear.blogspot.com

Two veteran teachers and published authors write reviews about books: children's books, books for teachers, and books related to children and/or education.

CHAPTER 10

Homeschool Blogs

Today there are many wonderful ways for children to be educated, and no one way is right for everyone. We are fortunate that we have so many options available, and at the same time have a sense of camaraderie and giving amongst educators in all situations. Like classroom teachers, homeschoolers are some of the most creative and generous people on the planet. They offer unique curriculum, printables, and tales from the trenches of parenting, working, keeping a home, and teaching multiple ages all day, every day!

For those of you who don't know any homeschoolers, forget about all of the stereotypes. Just like teachers and students, homeschoolers are all different. They come from all over—inner cities, suburbs, rural farms, foreign countries, and next door. Homeschoolers are stay-at-home mothers and fathers, working parents, work-at-home mothers and fathers, and grandparents. They have a high school diploma, or a college degree, or advanced graduate degrees. Some homeschool for religious reasons, others because of academic philosophies or because their child has special needs that are difficult to meet in a school setting. Many are teachers or former teachers themselves.

And lots of those talented homeschoolers have put together amazing resources that can easily be adapted for home or classroom use. The blogs included in this chapter can energize any teacher, whether you teach at a public school, private school, parochial school, or charter or magnet school—or you teach your own kids around your kitchen table. Look around and get to know these amazing bloggers, and get ready to have your best year of teaching ever!

1 + 1 + 1 = 1
http://1plus1plus1equals1.blogspot.com

Carisa homeschools her toddler (preschool), kindergartener, and third grader and is one of the most creative moms on the Internet. She taught kindergarten before her family moved into the inner city as missionaries. Now, she offers all of her creativity and innovative solutions to learning problems and motivation on this blog and its companion site. You'll find preschool and tot "packs" filled with downloadable skills sheets, worksheets, creative ideas she's compiled for working with her older son, and lots of great inspiration.

Blog, She Wrote
http://blogshewrote.blogspot.com

There are some great posts about the day-to-day education of the author's four kids and curriculum reviews on this blog. If you click on the unit studies link, you'll find booklists, projects, and activity ideas that go along with themes and books.

Bright Kids at Home
http://brightkidsathome.com

This is a collection of ideas and resources for those who decide to teach their gifted children at home.

Cajun Joie de Vivre
http://amybayliss.com

Amy Bayliss shares her take on getting the most out of life, staying organized, and homeschooling boys. You'll find wonderful printable organizers and forms at her blog.

Chocolate on My Cranium
http://chocolateonmycranium.blogspot.com

I love this blog. The author speaks in chocolate metaphors (who doesn't like that?) and shares a slice of her life as she and her husband raise their children and keep their farm going. There are great tutorials and lesson ideas. Under the homeschool tab, you'll find free unit plans and other resources.

Confessions of a Homeschooler
http://www.confessionsofahomeschooler.com

This is one of the most popular—and wonderful—homeschool blogs on the web! Erica is truly talented, creative, and generous. She homeschools four kids, writing much of her own curriculum. Some of it is available for a small fee, but most of it is available for free download. My kids and I have enjoyed every idea we've ever gotten from COAH.

Confessions of an Organized Homeschool Mom
http://www.bethanylebedz.blogspot.com

This blogger shares tips on organization that will benefit anyone—homeschooler, classroom teacher, overwhelmed mom, or overcommitted dad. She also reviews books and products.

Delightful Learning
http://delightfullearning.blogspot.com

I LOVE this blog! Every time I visit it, I come away with another great idea or inspiration. One of my favorite posts is an idea for little ones: L is for Lemonade and Ladybugs. Have the kids make lemon prints with yellow paint and lemon halves, fresh lemonade, fingerprint ladybugs, read about ladybugs for science, count spots on paper ladybugs, and other fun activities.

Discover Their Gifts
http://discovertheirgifts.blogspot.com

I love blogs that share lots of pictures of kids doing creative and interesting things. I also love to see ideas played out in the real world to figure out how they might work for me. This blog does a great job meeting those goals.

Eclectic Whatnot
http://www.eclecticwhatnot.com

I need to warn you . . . when you are ready to check out this blog, make sure you have time to hang out. Ruthanne is seriously hilarious. On a day when you are going crazy, whether it is from your homeschooling or classroom responsibilities or day-to-day life, venture on it and stay a while. You'll forget your troubles.

HOMESCHOOL BLOGS

A Familiar Path
http://afamiliarpath.com

This is a beautiful homeschooling blog about the simple things in life. It includes exquisite photographs, wonderful insights, and practical ideas.

Five J's: Striving to Raise Lifelong Learners
http://fivejs.com

This is such a resource-rich blog! The blogger shares articles, downloads, and tips for encouraging a love of learning in kids of all ages.

The Happy Housewife
http://thehappyhousewife.com

Check out "Happy's" blog for homeschooling ideas and tips, giveaways, homemaking support, frugal living advice, and more. This is a great blog, and one of the ones I make sure I read every day.

Homegrown Learners
http://www.homegrownlearners.com

Another former educator turned homeschool mom, this blogger has lots to share. Curriculum ideas, examples of things that worked and didn't, and lots of links can be found here.

The Homeschool Chick
http://www.thehomeschoolchick.com

This blog takes a light-hearted look at homeschooling and life. You'll find tips, tricks, recipes, and household management advice, along with encouragement.

Homeschool Creations
http://homeschoolcreations.blogspot.com

Homeschool Creations is one of the best education blogs around. Whether you homeschool or not, Jolanthe, the creative force behind it, has so many incredible ideas and offers them all to her readers for free. You'll find printables, creative lesson ideas, and reviews on products that are fun and educational for kids of all ages.

Homeschool Share
http://www.homeschoolshare.com

This site shares free printables, unit plans, and lap book pages for educators of all types to use with kids.

Homeschooling Belle
http://www.homeschoolingbelle.com

This homeschooling mom shares her family's untraditional stories, ideas for crafts and projects, and insights on life in general. A great blog to check out.

Jimmie's Collage
http://jimmiescollage.com

Jimmie shares advice, encouragement, and lots of free printables. This is definitely a blog to follow.

Journey to Excellence
http://journey2excellence.blogspot.com

Mom to four—two homeschooled, two public schooled—this blogger shares what each kid is doing and participates in several blog hops, so there are always links available to click and see what other bloggers are doing with the same subjects.

Let's Play Math
http://letsplaymath.net

This homeschooling mom has taught math to every level from pre-K to undergraduate physics, and loves the challenge of making math fun for her kids. She presents unique problems, offers reviews on math books and products, and gives great advice for how to teach math to any student.

A Little of This, a Little of That
http://alittleofthis---alittleofthat.blogspot.com

Fun and creative crafts and activities abound on this site. Creative classroom teachers can find inspiration to twist into a great school idea like the recently added (as I was writing this book, search the archives) "I Spy Bags." The creative force behind this blog sewed up a square bag with fun fabric and a clear plastic window, filled it with small themed buttons and white plastic pellets, and attached a card detailing what her son and daughter needed to find in the bags. This would be a fun, quiet classroom time-filler: Repurpose a water bottle by filling it with buttons and pellets and hot gluing the lid on. Attach your direction card, and let your primary students try to find all of the hidden items. Homeschool parents will find wonderful sewing and craft projects to make for and with their children.

Living the Chaotic Life
http://www.livingthechaoticlife.com

Mom to four kids, one with autism, Angela gives a great perspective on teaching kids with special needs, homeschooling, and advocacy for kids with disabilities and education.

Mama Jenn
http://mama-jenn.blogspot.com

Homeschooling mom to five kids (two sets of twins!) in preschool, first, and third grade, Mama Jenn shares many amazing craft, project, lesson, manipulative, and printable ideas on her blog that you really should check it out. I'm sure you'll be like me, every time I stop by, lost for an hour as I click back posts and embedded links to project instructions. One of my favorites is the car theme for her little preschoolers. We borrowed that idea over here, and my two youngest have had a lot of fun matching our extensive toy car collection to construction paper "parking lots," driving on number-shaped "roads," and making race cars out of recyclables.

Milk and Cookies
http://www.milkandcookiesblog.com

Mom and homeschooler to a son, this blogger shares insight on teaching to and living with a boy all day, every day.

The Moffat Girls
http://moffattgirls.blogspot.com

This elementary teacher turned homeschool mom creates and shares wonderful resources for Pre-K and kindergarten learners.

Mom 2 Three Adopted Sibs
http://mom2threeadoptedsibs.blogspot.com

This mom offers reviews of homeschooling curriculum and educational products and gives real-life examples of a mom teaching multiple ages.

My Home Sweet Home
http://myhomesweethomeonline.net

This is another blog filled with beautiful photographs and lots of day-to-day homeschooling advice and conversation about what works for the author's family.

Our Journey Westward
http://ourjourneywestward.com

Cindy West, a former elementary teacher, curriculum developer, and writer, homeschools her three children and blogs about their adventures, offers encouragement and curriculum ideas, and shares reviews.

Passport Academy
http://www.passportacademy.com

This blog is specifically devoted to homeschooling five kids. The blogger shares tips, resources, printables, and curriculum.

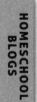

HOMESCHOOL BLOGS

Read-Aloud Dad
http://www.readalouddad.com

While the read-aloud dad is not technically a homeschooler (his twins aren't old enough for school and his blog chronicles what they are currently doing), I found him linked up on so many homeschoolers' blogs that I included his blog in this section. He reads constantly to his kids, and reviews every book he reads to them. On his "About" page he specifically states that he reviews only books that he buys (doesn't accept review copies from publishers or authors) because he wants to be able to say exactly what he and his kids thought of the book.

Rockin C

http://teaching2manydiligently.blogspot.com

Homeschooling four of their six children (all boys!) on an 800-acre cattle ranch certainly presents some unique challenges, but Tiffany provides a glimpse into making it all work with style and grace. Teachers and other homeschoolers can learn a lot from this blog.

Special Needs Homeschooling

http://specialneedshomeschooling.com

This blog offers great reviews and suggestions for homeschooling kids with special needs. This family has schooled everywhere—doctors' offices, hospitals, and therapy appointments. She has lots of great advice to offer.

Spell Outloud Homeschool

http://www.spelloutloud.com

Maureen Spell is a former elementary teacher and is now a homeschool mom to six kids. She shares reviews, tips for integrating meaningful play and learning activities with all kids throughout the day, and wonderful printables.

Stone Soup Homeschool Resources

http://www.stonesouphomeschool.com

This blog is loaded with resources for homeschool veterans and classroom teachers alike. Check out the resources categorized by subject area.

Sweet Phenomena

http://sweetphenomena.com

A homeschool mom "born out of necessity," as she calls it, Tiffany shares about curriculum, organizations, field trips, and more. She began homeschooling her daughter when an impending cross-country move brought up the possibility of her daughter being in three schools in one year! Since they began that rocky first year, their homeschool has blossomed into a rich learning environment . . . one they plan on sticking with for the duration of their daughter's schooling.

Teach Beside Me
http://teachbesideme.blogspot.com

This blog features lots of pictures and examples of how this family integrates learning into their everyday lives. It's fun to read, with lots of links.

Teaching With TLC
http://www.teachingwithtlc.com

A former elementary teacher and curriculum specialist, this blog and book author shares wonderful inspiration and resources for parents and teachers. There are free resources, as well as some priced at a few dollars each, available on this blog.

Totally Tots
http://totallytots.blogspot.com

Several creative homeschoolers contribute to this blog designed just for the teachers of our littlest students. There are fun ideas for developing themed sensory tubs and tables, alphabet and counting games, and themes galore. You'll also find activities to go along with favorite picture and concept books.

The Tuckers Take Tennessee
http://www.thetuckerstaketennessee.com

You'll find tutorials, reviews, and advice for homeschooling your kids on this site. The blogger is fun, down to Earth, and easy to read. I enjoy this site.

HOMESCHOOL BLOGS

CHAPTER 11

Conclusion

Teaching—whether you teach one or 50 students—can be overwhelming at the start of each year. You want your students to have every opportunity you can provide them. I hope you believe now that you *can* provide your students with a creative and full education without spending your hard-earned money.

Remember that you can find an incredible, awe-inspiring number of free resources with just a little effort. Think creatively before throwing the peanut butter jars and egg cartons away. Can one become a bug box? How about a math game? If you drill a few holes in the top of a peanut butter jar, scrape off the label, and wash it thoroughly, you will have a great bug box for your students to use when they go outside on a nature walk or to play on the playground! An egg carton is good for so many things. Recently, I wanted my daughter to brush up on one-to-one correspondence to help with her math. I took some round dot stickers, wrote a number on each (1–12), and stuck them one by one inside the sections in the carton. I put a little baggie of kidney beans in the carton, closed it up, and decorated the outside with some glue, ribbon, and scrapbook paper. My daughter loves to "bean count," putting one kidney bean in the section marked one, two in the two section, and so on. Easy, fun, and free!

The ideas are out there . . . have fun as you search. And get ready to enjoy your most creative season of teaching ever! Remember, if you come across a resource that you think is too great not to share, or you have an idea for a free or frugal project, drop me a line at resource@colleen-kessler.com. Check out my blog for additional freebies, project and activity ideas, and more: http://www.raisinglifelonglearners.com.

About the Author

Colleen Kessler is passionate about kids, hands-on learning, science, nature, gifted education, teaching, and books, and she indulges those passions every day as a science and education writer. Whether she is in her office overlooking her backyard, a National Wildlife Federation Certified Wildlife Habitat; taking a hike through the nearby meadows or woods; or trying out new experiments, activities, and projects for her books with her three kids, Colleen is learning all of the time.

She is always on the lookout for meaningful, engaging, and hands-on ideas to inspire a love of learning and intrinsic desire to find out more in kids of all ages. These ideas spark new ones, and the excitement goes on and on. She considers herself a lifelong learner and hopes to help others—teachers, parents, and kids—to see themselves that way, too.

Colleen has written textbook chapters, teacher resources, lessons, experiments, games, leveled readers, and more for numerous educational publishers. She is the author of science books including *Real-Life Science Mysteries*, *Hands-On Ecology*, and *Super Smart Science* from Prufrock Press, and seven books in the A Project Guide series from Mitchell Lane.

When Colleen is not writing, she can often be found speaking to kids and teachers, or presenting at workshops, conferences, or schools about education, science, and writing. Or . . . you might find her out scooping monarch chrysalises, setting off soda-pop geysers, or swinging in the park with the kids.

For more free resources, ideas for simple ways to engage kids in learning, and information on her writing and her adventures homeschooling her twice-exceptional son, gifted daughter, and havoc-wreaking toddler, check out Colleen's blog: http://www.raisinglifelonglearners.com. You can learn more about Colleen and her books on her website at http://www.colleen-kessler.com. She can be contacted at colleen@colleen-kessler.com.